Royal
Horticultural
Society

Carol Klein's

GROW YOUR OWN

VEG

Journal

First published in Great Britain in 2008
by Mitchell Beazley, an imprint of
Octopus Publishing Group Ltd,
2–4 Heron Quays, London E14 4JP
An Hachette Livre Company
www.octopusbooks.co.uk

Published in association with the
Royal Horticultural Society

Reprinted 2009 (twice)

ISBN 978-1-84533-471-0

A CIP record of this book is available from
the British Library

Mitchell Beazley
Commissioning editor Helen Griffin
Editorial director Tracey Smith
Art director Tim Foster
Art editor Victoria Burley
Project editor Ruth Patrick
Production manager Peter Hunt

Royal Horticultural Society
Publisher Susannah Charlton
Commissioning editor Rae Spencer-Jones

Created and produced for Mitchell Beazley
by The Bridgewater Book Company Ltd
Creative director Peter Bridgewater
Editorial director Tom Kitch
Project editor Jane Courtier
Editor Emily Bailey
Designers Bernard Higton and Virginia Zeal
Picture research Liz Eddison
Indexer Shirley May

Set in Frutiger, Glypha, Interstate and Rage

Colour reproduction by United Graphics,
Singapore
Printed and bound by Toppan, China

The Royal Horticultural Society is the UK's
leading gardening charity dedicated to
advancing horticulture and promoting
good gardening. Its charitable work
includes providing expert advice and
information, training the next generation
of gardeners, creating hands-on
opportunities for children to grow plants
and conducting research into plants,
pests and environmental issues affecting
gardeners. For more information, visit:
www.rhs.org.uk or call 0845 130 4646.

Contents

		VEG OF THE MONTH	RECIPE OF THE MONTH
January	6	Leeks 10	Colcannon 12
February	20	Jerusalem Artichokes 24	Curried parsnip soup 26
March	34	Broccoli 38	Leek and spinach filo triangles 40
April	48	Spinach 52	Spinach roulade 54
May	64	Broad Beans 68	Hot asparagus with balsamic vinegar 70
June	80	Carrots 84	Pea, lettuce and lemon soup 86
July	96	Beetroot 100	Beetroot salad with coriander and tomato salsa 102
August	112	Tomatoes 116	Stuffed peppers 118
September	128	Sweetcorn 132	Fresh vegetable pizza 134
October	144	Pumpkins 148	Green tomato chutney 150
November	158	Celeriac 162	Roasted root vegetable and pumpkin tart 164
December	172	Turnip 176	Buttered cauliflower crumble 178

Resources 184 I Sowing and harvesting charts 186 I Glossary 188 I Conversion charts 190 I Index 191

Starting to grow your own

" Growing your own food is a labour of love. You know exactly how it has been produced and that it has the lowest possible carbon footprint on its journey from your garden to the table. You can enjoy vegetables that taste more delicious than anything you could ever buy from a shop or restaurant, packed full of goodness and as fresh as can be. You can choose varieties for their flavour and culinary qualities rather than their blandness and uniformity. Plunging your hands into the soil to plant the first potatoes, carefully sowing seed and later harvesting the bounty your plot has produced is not just satisfying, it is a reminder of our part in a hugely important activity that has been practised by our forebears from time immemorial.

From this common history comes a shared experience, but embarking on growing your own for the first time can nonetheless be daunting, When can I sow my first carrots? How many courgette plants do I need? Does it matter which way up these seeds go? And even the more experienced gardener will still appreciate a timely reminder about when to sow, stake or harvest. Planning and organizing the vegetable plot and the jobs that need doing in it are essential to success. If we are to avoid gluts and famines, crops must be sown at the right time and in the right amounts. When do we dig, incorporate manure or start a compost heap?

The smaller the garden, the more vital it is to make full use of the space. I garden organically and try to ensure the health of the soil and their crops using companion planting, rotation and observation. No scheme is foolproof – conditions vary radically in different parts of the country and from garden to garden; the weather will be unpredictable. But I hope this journal will suggest and remind you of what to do when, wherever you live and whatever you grow. Happy gardening. "

JANUARY

" Though freezing weather may make it impossible to do much work, this is still a busy time. There is compost to turn, muck to be spread and new beds to build. And there is seed to be sown. Bright window ledges are useful, cold frames and greenhouses are a huge bonus – especially with simple insulation to keep up the temperatures – but ones with a bit of heat vastly broaden the vegetable grower's scope. Seed of tender crops can be started early – I sometimes sow my tomatoes before the end of the month, giving them a flying start. Salad crops can be started and harvested throughout the winter with the minimum of heat, and though they take longer to grow than at the height of summer, the benefits are obvious – fresh green crops, such as supplies of lettuce rocket, mizuna and various mustards will go on and on. We use them as a cut-and-come again crop. With the protection of a piece of horticultural fleece or a cloche, the same crops sown outside in September will continue to yield through until the spring. Even in fiercely cold weather, lamb's lettuce (or mache) will recover as soon as temperatures rise above freezing – no wonder this has been a mainstay salad crop in continental Europe for centuries. Frozen herbs, such as basil, mint, parsley, dill and chervil can all be crumbled into winter dishes to give a taste of the spring, but this is the season to enjoy hearty root vegetables, dip into jars of peas and beans and bake pumpkins and winter squash until they yield their soft, golden flesh. "

Jobs for January

Continue harvesting winter vegetables Brussels sprouts, leeks, parsnips, swede, turnips, celeriac, cabbage, cauliflower and kale are among the crops available now.

Make early sowings indoors If you can't wait to get going, broad beans, lettuce, summer cabbages and spinach can be sown in pots or modules in a warm greenhouse or sunroom, though waiting until next month might give more reliable results.

Continue setting out seed potatoes Old egg boxes make useful containers for potato tubers set out to chit. Most of the shoots on a tuber usually come from one end, the 'rose end' – you can see which end it is because it will have most of the 'eyes'. Set the tubers with this end uppermost.

Sow onions January is the traditional time to sow onions to obtain large bulbs. Keep the seedlings warm and in a bright position; plant them out in March.

Take care with soil Don't cultivate heavy soil when it is sodden – you will destroy the soil structure. The test is that you should be able to walk across the soil without it clinging stickily to your boots. Lay a broad wooden plank as a walkway where you need to cross the soil to access your crops – this spreads the load and reduces the damage.

Protect cauliflowers Snap the stem of one of the outside leaves of a cauliflower without breaking it off completely, so that the leaf can be bent over the cauliflower curd to protect it from cold weather. It will also keep the sun off, helping to prevent the creamy white florets yellowing.

Warm the soil Set out cloches or polythene over areas of soil marked out for early sowings. This does not so much trap the heat as allow the soil to dry out, thereby raising the temperature. It also makes the soil workable that much sooner.

Check brassica netting In cold weather, pigeons will be increasingly likely to damage brassica crops. They can do a huge amount of damage very quickly, stripping the leaves from the plants. Check that netting or fleece covers are still in place.

Seek out slugs Check under the lower leaves of crops for slugs and snails, and remove any that you find.

Week 1

> **Growing and eating your own is immensely good for the soul – therapeutic in every way**

Leeks

Versatile and useful, leeks are easy to grow in the right soil conditions. They may occupy the ground for a long while, but the great advantage is that they can be harvested from autumn right through to late winter.

Leek tips
• Grow in moisture-retentive soil that doesn't become waterlogged in winter.
• For an early crop to mature from late summer to autumn, sow in a seed tray from mid- to late winter in a heated greenhouse or on a windowsill, planting out in mid-spring.
• For the main winter crop, sow outside in a seedbed from mid-spring to midsummer. Transplant when the young plants are about pencil thick.

• Plant leeks into wide, deep holes – 15cm (6in) deep and 5cm (2in) across – dropping a single seedling in each. Don't backfill with soil, but simply fill each hole with water to settle the soil around the roots.

Recommended varieties
'Carlton' AGM: Early-maturing, strong-growing and tasty. Seeds germinate quickly and yields are high.
'Apollo' AGM: High yields from December. A blue-green leek with good resistance to rust.
'Toledo' AGM: High-yielding with long, white shafts. Crops late in the season.
'Pancho' AGM: A good early yield of rust-resistant, tasty leeks with long, solid shafts.

Week 2

Colcannon

Cabbage is much maligned – in fact, it has probably had the worst press of any vegetable. Banish pungent memories of school cabbage, boiled to disintegration, with this traditional Irish recipe.

Ingredients

Serves 4

500g (1lb) potatoes
500g (1lb) kale or green leaf cabbage, stalk removed, finely shredded
6 spring onions, finely chopped
150ml (¼ pint) milk or cream
125g (4oz) butter
salt and pepper

Method

Put the potatoes on to boil in a pan of lightly salted water. You can either peel the potatoes before cooking, or boil them in their skins and peel them once cooked – this is the traditional Irish way.

While the potatoes are cooking, place the shredded cabbage or kale in a small amount of boiling water or a steamer and cook until just tender – don't overcook. Place the spring onions and the milk or cream in a pan and simmer over a low heat for about 5 minutes.

Drain the potatoes and mash. Add the hot milk mixture and half the butter, beating well to give a soft fluffy texture. Beat in the kale or cabbage; the colcannon should be a lovely speckled green. Season with salt and pepper and serve in individual bowls. Make a well in the centre of each mound and put a knob of the remaining butter in each one. Serve immediately.

Week 3

> **Take time to get to know your soil: it is the raw material of vegetable growing**

Chitting potatoes

Above: Set seed potatoes in a bright place so that they develop sturdy sprouts before planting.

Getting potatoes started couldn't be easier. Just as in the supermarket you buy potatoes off the shelf, here the difference is that the ones you sow are special 'seed' potatoes – certifiably free from viruses.

Usually they come in small bags, available from late winter, which may contain more potatoes than you need. In this case, share the purchase with a friend, or club in with others so that you can grow smaller quantities of a more diverse range of varieties. This way, you will discover much more quickly which varieties you prefer to eat, and which ones grow best in your soil.

Growing an early crop

Everyone looks forward to digging those first, delicious new potatoes of the season in early summer. To get your crop as soon as possible, choose those varieties which have a short growing season; the so-called called 'first earlies' and 'second earlies'. A tasty first early is 'Accent', with creamy, waxy flesh; among the second earlies are smooth-skinned 'Kestrel' and long, oval 'Lady Christl'.

Once you have bought your seed potatoes, start them into growth by sprouting, or chitting, them four to six weeks before planting. The advantage of doing this is that it gets them into early growth, ready for the season ahead.

Set the tubers on end, with their 'eyes' uppermost, in egg boxes or seed trays, and place in good light in a cool room. Each potato will develop several sturdy green shoots. If the tubers are not in a bright enough place, the shoots that develop will be long, pale and rather fragile, and prone to being accidentally knocked off at planting time.

Another trick for achieving the earliest crops is to accelerate growth by increasing the soil temperature of the planting area by covering it with black plastic several weeks before planting. You can plant the potatoes through holes made in the plastic.

Plant your seed potatoes from early to late spring. Remember that potato shoots are very sensitive to cold; if a frost is forecast once the shoots are showing through the soil, draw soil right over their tops to protect them. You can add a layer of fleece or straw, or even sheets of newspaper, for additional insulation.

Week 4

Preparing your plot

Soil is the raw material of vegetable growing. Before you decide what you want to grow in it, you need to know a little bit about your soil.

Identifying the elements

Roll some topsoil between your hands. If it flakes and crumbles, it is low in clay. If it feels gritty between finger and thumb, it is sandy. A soapy or silky feel suggests silt, and if it is easy to roll into a sausage shape, it is clay.

Clay is rich in nutrients, drains poorly in the winter and is slow to warm up in spring. But it is usually moist in the summer, and can grow good crops of most vegetables.

Sandy soil drains easily in winter and warms up quickly in spring, but holds few nutrients and dries out in summer. It is good for early crops, but later ones often need watering.

Loam lies in between clay and sand. This all too rare soil combines most of the best features of clay and sand.

Silt behaves like loam but is easily smeared and damaged in winter. It is very fertile but rarely found in gardens.

Soil structure

Soils consist of minerals, clay, sand and silt, which are coated in and bound by organic materials to produce small lumps or crumbs that give structure to the soil. The air spaces between these lumps allow oxygen, water and roots to enter the soil.

Working or trampling on your soil, especially when it is wet, ruins the crumb structure. On the other hand, digging in well-rotted organic matter such as garden compost or manure, applying mulches of organic matter, and working your soil only when it is reasonably dry, preserves and enhances the soil structure and improves crops.

Top left: Prepare your soil by breaking it up and removing weeds from it with a cultivator.

Top right: Digging in plenty of organic matter will help to achieve soil that is easy to cultivate and breaks down to fine crumbs for seed sowing.

Bottom: Good quality soil is vital for producing heavy crops of vegetables.

ACID OR ALKALINE?

Measuring the pH of your soil enables you to determine whether the soil is acid or alkaline. Although a laboratory test is best (and not hugely expensive), soil test kits are available from all good gardening stores. A pH of 7 is neutral, less than 7 is acid and more than 7 is alkaline. Vegetables grow best in a slightly acid soil with a pH of 6.5, although pH 7–7.5 helps reduce club root disease in the cabbage family. Acid soils can easily be made more alkaline by the application of garden lime.

Seasonal check

This is a good time to make sure you have sufficient supplies of everything you are likely to need through the busy weeks ahead, and that all your equipment is clean and tidy, and in good order.

Buy in plenty of seed compost ready for the sowing season; if this can be stored in a greenhouse, it will give it a chance to warm up and get seeds off to a flying start. Seed trays and pots should be checked and made sparkling clean. Damaged containers should be replaced. Plastic propagator tops for seed trays and pots are very useful but can have a short life, so replace these where necessary, too. Make sure any heated propagators are working properly.

Any existing packs of fertilizers or garden chemicals that have become damp, or lost their labels or instructions, should be safely disposed of (ask your local council for advice) and suitable new products bought.

If you will be using a greenhouse for plant raising, clear out any debris, brush down the framework with a stiff brush, and wash the glass to rid it of grime and allow maximum light transmission.

If you have not already ordered your seeds, do so now. Gardening centres usually stock a reasonable supply, but mail order seed catalogues will give you much more choice.

Tool store

Check that your tools are clean and in good condition. It may be time to invest in some new or extra tools: having the right tools for the job, and plenty of them, makes growing vegetables much easier and leaves more time for you to enjoy the end result. Good inexpensive tools are sold by DIY or garden stores and are widely available second hand. Make sure you clean your tools and store them carefully after every use. That way they will last longer and be a pleasure to use every time.

Essential tools for growing your own vegetables include:
• a spade and fork
• a push or draw hoe
• a trowel and hand fork
• a rake
• a pair of secateurs
• a hose pipe
• a watering can
• boots and gloves

Left: Having the right tools will make gardening easier and more enjoyable.

Above right: Check that containers are clean and ready for the start of the growing season.

FEBRUARY

" February days can be bitter, and the cold
seems to accumulate. The fact that the
ground has been subjected to prolonged
periods of frost seems to make it colder still.
For some vegetables though, the cold means
improvement. Parsnips left in the ground taste
sweeter after frost. So too do Jerusalem artichokes.
Much of their starch changes to sugar.

Storing vegetables is an art that has almost died
out with the advent of year-round supermarket
produce. A wonderful woman we talked to for *Grow
Your Own Veg* dug trenches on her allotment, lifted
root veg and and buried them for the winter, turfing
them out as and when required. Earth is the best insulation.

Anyone who has a bright windowsill can start off sprouted seed
at any time and it is surely now that these small shoots and leaves,
packed with vitality, are most treasured. Seeds of almost anything
can be started now – beetroot and broccoli are good, as well as
the usual salad candidates. Pea sprouts are a delicious addition
to a stir-fry.

In the garden, areas of soil can be designated and covered with
recycled black polythene to warm and dry out the soil for early
crops. Glass cloches are actually the most effective means to warm
the soil but the polythene method is effective and cheap.
As the month progresses, it becomes easier to imagine
growth sprouting, and suddenly it is about to happen. **"**

Jobs for February

Waiting for spring By late winter, there is an almost irresistible temptation to start sowing and planting, and you can safely begin sowing early crops in the greenhouse or on a sunny windowsill. Broad beans, Brussels sprouts, early summer cabbage, calabrese, cauliflowers, leeks, onions, peas, radishes, shallots, spinach and turnips can all be raised under cover. Windowsills are often rather dark and seedlings suffer if grown on them for prolonged periods. Greenhouses offer better conditions, but some heating is needed to produce healthy, well-grown plants. Unless your garden is unusually well-drained and in a sheltered, mild district, wait for the warm weather of spring before planting anything.

Buying plants It is sometimes more convenient to buy plants in spring than to take the trouble of raising your own early transplants. Check the catalogues – most of the major seed suppliers offer plug plants. Order early to be sure of getting what you want.

Finish digging The sooner digging and incorporation of compost or manure is finished now, the better.

Start preparing seedbeds If the weather is dry, start raking down the soil to prepare seedbeds. The soil needs to be broken down into fine, even crumbs; if the frost has not broken down all the clods, tap them smartly with the back of a fork or rake to shatter.

Continue forcing Rhubarb, chicory and seakale can all continue to be forced this month.

Sow outside in mild gardens
In sheltered gardens in mild areas, the first sowings can often be made outside towards the end of this month. Light, free-draining soil is necessary. Broad beans, carrots, beetroot, onions, lettuces, radish, first early peas, spinach and summer cabbage are worth trying if the conditions are right.

Feed spring greens Spring cabbages are now hearting up, and a high nitrogen feed will help them produce a good crop.

Lift parsnips Parsnips left in the ground will soon start into growth again, making the roots flabby. Lift remaining parsnips and use them up before the spring weather arrives.

Sow greenhouse crops Tomatoes, aubergines, peppers, melons and cucumbers for cropping in the greenhouse can be sown now, in a warm propagator.

Week 1

Jerusalem Artichokes

The knobbly tubers of the Jerusalem artichoke make a delicious vegetable. It is extraordinarily productive even in poor soil, and requires the minimum amount of work.

Jerusalem artichoke tips

• Although they prefer sun and well-drained, moisture-retentive soil, they will tolerate heavy, shady and dry sites, such as under trees and near hedges, where other crops won't grow.
• Plants grow up to 3m (10ft) high, so need careful positioning because of the shade they cast – though they will also form a useful windbreak.
• When the stems die back in late autumn, cut them back to 15cm (6in) above the soil. The tubers will survive perfectly well in the ground, but over winter it is best to provide a mulch of old stems, straw or newspaper to protect them.
• If you don't want any Jerusalem artichokes next year, make sure that you dig them all – even the smallest – out of the ground or they'll regrow.
• Guard against slugs and snails, which can hollow out tubers and like to eat the young shoots.

Recommended varieties

'Fuseau': Long, relatively smooth tubers make this variety easy to prepare in the kitchen. Slightly smoky taste.
'Stampede': An early-maturing variety with large tubers that have a very good texture and flavour.

Week 2

> **In a good year,
the monumental stems
of Jerusalem artichokes
are decked in bright
yellow flowers**

Curried parsnip soup

Parsnips and spices are blended to create a warming soup with an Indian flavour. If you prefer a milder flavour, use less curry powder or choose a milder version.

Ingredients

Serves 6

125g (4oz) butter
1.5kg (3lb) parsnips, scrubbed and
   roughly chopped
1 onion, chopped
1 potato, chopped
1 tablespoon medium hot curry powder
1 teaspoon ground turmeric
½ teaspoon ground cumin
1.8 litres (3 pints) vegetable stock
150ml (¼ pint) double cream
salt and pepper
snipped chives or finely chopped parsley,
   to garnish

Method

Melt the butter in a large, heavy-based saucepan. Add the parsnips, onion, potato, curry powder, turmeric and cumin and stir well. Cover and cook over a low to moderate heat, stirring occasionally, for 10 minutes.

Add the stock and bring to the boil. Reduce the heat, cover and simmer for 30 minutes. Add a little water if the soup is too thick.

In a blender or food processor, blend the soup in batches, then transfer it to a clean saucepan. Reheat gently and stir in the cream. Serve the soup immediately in warm soup bowls, garnishing each portion with a sprinkling of chives or parsley.

Week 3

Improving your soil

Above: Adding organic matter to soil helps to improve its structure.

Fertile conditions boost the size, flavour, yield and quality of your vegetables. If you can, add bulky, well-rotted organic matter, such as garden compost or farmyard manure, every second or third year to half or one-third of your plot.

Bulky organic matter adds fibrous humus as well as nutrients to the soil. Humus absorbs water so that it remains available to plants. It allows free-draining soil to hold on to moisture longer, and improves drainage in heavy clay soil, so it's great for any soil type.

Some crops, such as carrots and parsnips, are best grown on soil that was manured the previous year, as their roots tend to fork and become misshapen on freshly manured soil.

As a rough guide, one bucketful of well-rotted material to every square metre is enough for most soils.

Green manures

Special crops can be grown just to improve the soil. Grown in autumn or over winter, when the ground is otherwise bare, green manures stop nutrients from being washed out by rain. They won't add much nutrient value to the soil but they do save nutrients, reduce potential pollution and make the soil more workable.

Cut down green manures while their stems are still soft. Chop the topgrowth up to help it decompose, and allow it to wilt for a few days before digging it in.

• Sow mustard or fodder radish in late summer as the main crops are being harvested and removed.

• Sow vetches or tares and rye in early autumn and allow to grow over winter, before digging them in during early spring at least two weeks before sowing the next year's crops.

CAROL'S GREEN TIP

Municipal compost

Many councils now provide households with a separate bin for compostable material, which is collected along with the rest of your recyclables. This is turned into compost and sold back to householders, usually at a reasonable price. It's a great idea if you don't have enough room for your own compost heap. Many councils also sell home composters, often at a reduced cost.

Week **4**

> **When you grow your own you know exactly what's in and on your vegetables**

Choosing your crops and buying your seed

Since you can't grow everything you want in a small vegetable plot, stick to your favourite vegetables and those in which freshness really counts. Do you really want to grow crops that are readily available, cheap and tasty in the shops? It's probably better to concentrate on those that are expensive or difficult to buy, or ones that taste so much better eaten within minutes of picking.

Decide how much time and effort you are able to devote to caring for your vegetables; select easy-care crops if you know you will be too busy to devote time to lots of regular maintenance.

Once you have made a list of what you like, decide how much you need. Remember that growing too little is better than growing too much and then having to discard produce that you have spent time and money nurturing.

Don't forget your soil type must be taken into account. Light soil warms up quickly in spring and is great for producing early crops. Cold, heavy clay, on the other hand, is slow to warm up, making early crops tricky to grow, but later crops should be abundant and will need relatively little watering.

Left: There is nothing to beat the pleasure of harvesting well-grown crops that all the family will appreciate.

Above right: In a small plot, it's important to concentrate on growing those crops that you really like.

Obtaining seed

Check the catalogues and websites of suppliers of vegetable seeds and plug plants. Most catalogues come out in late summer, giving you plenty of time to browse and get in an early order. Since seed can be stored in cool, dark, dry conditions, it is worth buying in as wide a selection as you have room for, saving surplus seed for future years. Seed packets usually have some kind of expiry date and, though it is true that old seeds are less likely to germinate than new ones, most are likely to be viable for several years, though leeks, onions and parnips are worth buying fresh each year.

To help you choose vegetables, the RHS regularly tests different kinds and publishes lists of recommended varieties on its website (www.rhs.org.uk/plants), giving its Award of Garden Merit (AGM) to the very best. AGM plants do not require highly specialist growing conditions or care.

Planning the year's cropping

Once you have decided what vegetables you want to grow, it is time to plan the year's cropping. Make a note of the harvest times of each crop. Ideally you want to plan for crops that will give you something to pick at every season of the year.

Successional sowings

Repeated sowing at intervals, called 'successional sowing', is necessary for a continuous supply of crops such as peas, beans, lettuces and cauliflowers. If you sow no more than you are likely to need over a two-week period each time, and then start again when the first plants are about 5–8cm (2–3½in) high, you will avoid waste and seldom be without produce.

Intercropping and catch cropping

Some vegetables grow quite slowly, and you can use the space between the developing plants to grow another quick-maturing crop before they need the space. For example, peas sown in mid-spring won't use up all their space or cast much shade until early summer. In the meantime, lettuces, spinach and rocket can be grown between the rows of peas. This is known as 'intercropping'.

Where a crop is gathered early, or planted late, there are opportunities to grow another crop before or after. This is called 'catch cropping'. So, broad beans sown in late winter can be cleared away in midsummer, leaving time for a row of French beans (in southern areas) to be sown for use in the autumn. Leeks planted out in midsummer leave time for a row of lettuces to be planted in early spring, which will be gathered before the leeks need setting out.

Top: Careful planning will help to make best use of the space in a small vegetable plot.

Bottom: Use the space between slow-growing sweetcorn plants to sow a quick crop of radishes.

ROTATION OF CROPS

Different crops suffer from different types of pests and diseases. If you grow the same crop in the same piece of soil year after year, soil-borne pests and diseases will have a chance to build up, and particular soil nutrients are likely to become exhausted. The way to avoid this is to rotate your crops. Divide your crops into three groups – root vegetables, brassicas, and everything else. Divide the plot into three equal sections, and move each group of crops forward to the next section each year.

MARCH

"Spring is here, and although it may not always be apparent, the season's inexorable push shows itself in new ways every day until, by the end of the month, its progress is undeniable. Buds swell and snowdrops are a thing of the past, as daffodils and all the little blue bulbs – scillas, chionodoxa and muscari – bring pools of colour to the dank earth. Broad beans and autumn-sown peas push forth – suddenly everything is happening.

There are seeds to be sown, but there is still ground to be dug over and raked. Now is the time to sow green manure – even in small patches where nothing will be put out for months, perhaps where sweetcorn, courgettes or tomatoes will be planted later – it can be sown now and throughout the growing year. Though it may only occupy the ground for a few months, it will stop nutrients leaching away, keep out weeds and add to the soil's fertility when dug in.

Whether it is the new shoots of clover or phacelia in the open ground or the first magical cotyledon leaves of cabbage or lettuce pushing their way through the compost, I still get the same thrill that possessed me when I first saw a seed germinate. From a tiny speck, new life surges forward. Eventually it will become a plant in its own right, and thinned out, weeded around and nurtured, it will grow strong and burgeon to give us food. Alongside these new crops, old faithfuls from last year are still yielding an important harvest. Leeks, broccoli, winter cabbage and kale and my all-time favourite – chard – are beginning to grow away again."

Jobs for March

Make a clean start Fork over the soil and double check that old crops and weeds have been removed.

Keep weeds at bay Hoe young weeds the moment they appear. It is worth preparing the seedbed just to encourage weed seeds to germinate so that you can kill them now. Once the surface weed seeds have germinated and been removed, few others will sprout and you will have a clean bed.

Rake the soil As soon as the soil is dry enough, rake it level and create a fine tilth.

Early feeding Most vegetable gardens need feeding. Once the winter rains have stopped, spread general-purpose fertilizer according to the pack directions.

Germination rates The soil is still often rather cold yet for good results. If in doubt, wait until weeds begin to emerge; when they germinate, so will your seed. It is better to wait a week or two than to sow in poor conditions.

Cover the soil To keep the soil weed-free and moist, ready for sowing, cover it with black polythene.

Prepare containers Fill containers with compost, ready for sowing.

Sow crops for transplanting Raise Brussels sprouts, leeks, summer cabbages and cauliflowers in pots or cell trays indoors, or in an outdoor seedbed.

Sow outdoors Broad beans, early carrots, calabrese, lettuces, onions, parsley, parsnips, peas, scorzonera, radishes, rocket, salsify, spinach, spring onions, turnips and herbs such as dill and chervil, can all be sown where they are to grow. If frost and winds are a problem, cover the area with fleece or cloches.

Carrots and cabbages All carrot and cabbage-related crops benefit from a fleece covering to exclude soil pests, cabbage root fly and carrot fly, which are on the wing in mid-spring.

Sow crops indoors Ideally in a greenhouse, or in the home, sow aubergines, beetroot, celeriac, celery, peppers (including chillies), tomatoes and tender herbs (such as basil).

Plant crowns, tubers and sets Plant asparagus crowns, tubers of early potatoes and Jerusalem artichokes, and onion sets and shallots.

Order young plants If you have decided not to raise your own plants from seed, order plug plants from mail-order suppliers as early as possible.

Guard against pests Apply slug controls to protect seedlings. The sudden disappearance of pea and bean seed indicates the presence of mice, so they will need to be trapped. Nets will help exclude birds from seedbeds, where they can be very destructive.

Week 1

Broccoli

Both white and purple sprouting broccoli stand for months right through the hardest days of winter, offering a crop of tight, crunchy heads at the end of winter into the early days of spring.

Broccoli tips

• Broccoli likes full sun and a rich soil with a pH of 6.5–7.5 (see page 16).
• Sow sprouting broccoli in seedbeds or modules from mid-spring to midsummer, ready for transplanting when they are roughly 10–15cm (4–6in) high.
• Broccoli needs firm planting, so don't be afraid to use your feet to firm the plants round the base of the stems.
• Leave 45cm (18in) between plants and rows. The wide spacing will ensure good air circulation around the plants and help prevent diseases.
• Pick the shoots regularly, before the flowers start to open. Frequent picking encourages side-shoot formation to extend the harvest.
• Check plants for signs of caterpillars and pick off by hand.

Recommended varieties

'Rudolph': A very early purple-sprouting variety that starts to produce its large, tasty spears from midwinter.
'Red Arrow' AGM: Heavy crops of claret-purple florets on tall stems over a long, late-winter season.
'White Star': Creamy white flowerheads of a delicate flavour, cropping in March and April.

Week 2

> **Fresh vegetables full of flavour all year round should be the ultimate aim of growing your own**

Leek and spinach filo triangles

Use up your leeks in early spring – soon they will form flower stems, spoiling their eating quality.

Ingredients

Serves 7 (makes 14 triangles)
250g (8oz) fresh spinach
75g (3oz) butter
65g (2½oz) finely chopped onion
2 garlic cloves, finely chopped
75g (3oz) thinly sliced leek
40g (1½oz) crumbled feta cheese
40g (1½oz) ricotta cheese
pinch freshly grated nutmeg
pepper
1 small egg, beaten
14 sheets fresh filo pastry, each
    31 x 18cm (12½ x 7in)
flat leaf parsley sprigs, to garnish
thick natural yogurt, to serve

Method

Preheat the oven to 190°C/375°F/gas mark 5. Wash the spinach, remove any tough stalks and shake to dry.

Heat half the butter in a large saucepan and fry the onion, garlic and leek until soft. Add the spinach and stir to combine. Cook over a moderate heat for 5–8 minutes until the spinach has wilted and is tender and all the liquid has evaporated, stirring when necessary. Squeeze the spinach mixture to remove any excess moisture, leave to cool, then stir in the feta, ricotta, nutmeg, pepper and beaten egg.

Melt the remaining butter and brush each filo sheet with it. Work with one filo sheet at a time, keeping the rest covered with plastic food wrap and a damp cloth. Fold each filo sheet in half lengthways and place 1 tablespoon of the spinach mixture on a short end. Fold the corners over the filling until you have a triangle with a small flap to tuck underneath. Brush with a little more butter and place on an oiled baking sheet.

Bake in the oven for 25–35 minutes until golden brown. Garnish with herbs and serve warm with yogurt.

Week 3

Sowing seeds for early crops

Above: Sowing seed under cover will give plants a head start in early spring.

Raising strong and healthy seedlings is a critical part of growing your own veg – all good crops depend on a good start, after all. To produce the earliest crops, some vegetables need to be started off when the weather is too cold for sowing outside, so they are sown in containers under cover – a greenhouse is ideal but a sun room, conservatory or even a windowsill can be put to good use.

Containers for sowing

Seeds can either be sown in trays or pots. There are also 'modules' – plastic trays divided into a number of individual pots. These are useful for minimizing root disturbance when planting out later.

Sowing technique

Use a sterile, bagged compost for seed sowing in containers; garden soil is not suitable. Fill the trays or pots with compost, pushing it well into the corners, and use a 'presser' (a piece of wood cut to fit the tray or pot) to strike the compost off level and firm it down lightly. Water the compost using a watering can fitted with a fine rose. Allow to drain before sowing the seed thinly, then cover with an even layer of more compost shaken through a small garden sieve. Cover with a propagator lid and a sheet of newspaper to keep off direct sun, and set in an evenly warm place to germinate.

When growing tender plants such as sweetcorn, runner beans and courgettes that cannot be planted out until all risk of frost is over, be careful not to sow too early under cover, or plants will get over-large and leggy before it is safe to plant them out. April is soon enough.

Below: The gentle warmth of a greenhouse helps to ensure you end up with healthy seedlings.

Week 4

> **There is something immensely satisfying about pushing a seed into compost and a few days later seeing a shoot thrusting its way out**

Greenhouse crops

A greenhouse can not only be used to give plants a head start while it is cold outside, but it also offers the extra warmth necessary for tender crops that prefer a long, warm season.

Aubergines Sow eight to ten seeds per 9cm (3½in) pot at 21–30°C (70–86°F). Move to individual pots when they are large enough to handle, and grow on at 16–18°C (61–64°F). Pinch out the growing tips once plants reach 30cm (12in), and plant out when the first flowers form, two or three per standard sized growing bag, one per 30cm (12in) pot.

Peppers Sow at 20°C (68°F) and transfer into individual 9cm (3½in) pots when large enough. Grow on at 18°C (64°F). When the roots fill the pot, plant out into growing bags or pots filled with multi-purpose compost.

Left: A frost-free greenhouse is perfect for raising plants in early spring, but also for growing tender crops to maturity.

Cucumbers In a greenhouse heated to a constant minimum temperature of 21°C (70°F), sow seeds now; in an unheated greenhouse, sow in late spring. Set the seeds on edge to prevent rotting, 1cm (½in) deep in small pots of moist seed compost. Once the first true leaves have expanded, move to 13cm (5in) pots and plant out four to five weeks after sowing.

Melons Sow at 20–25°C (68–77°F), placing one seed per 9cm (3½in) pot. Grow on at 18–20°C (64–68°F). In late spring, plant in growing bags (two per standard-sized bag) or in pots of multi-purpose compost, with one plant per 30cm (12in) pot.

Tomatoes Sow seeds thinly in pots or trays of moist seed compost at 20°C (68°F). Pot them up individually into 8cm (3½in) pots as soon as they are large enough to handle, and grow on at 18°C (64°F). Plant out when they are around 15–23cm (6–9in) tall, spacing them 45cm (18in) apart in the border, or two per growing bag.

WITHOUT A GREENHOUSE

While a greenhouse gives more reliable results, certain varieties of tender crops can be grown successfully outside. Choose a warm, very sheltered position, and make use of cloches and fleece to protect the plants in their early stages. To warm the soil, cover the planting area with polythene for at least six weeks in advance.

Planning a herb patch

Herbs are beautiful plants, often as lovely to look at as they are useful in the kitchen. Most herbs are from Mediterranean countries and prefer warm, dry conditions. The aromas they give off are most concentrated when they are grown in poor soils; moist, fertile conditions lead to lusher but less aromatic growth. So plant herbs in a sunny, open spot in free-draining, not-too-fertile soil; add some grit or sharp sand if you think the drainage needs to be improved.

There are a few exceptions to this rule: lovage, angelica, chervil, sorrel and sweet cicely are leafy plants that need semi-shaded, moist conditions to grow well. But the popular aromatic herbs like rosemary, thyme, sage and savory will thrive in thin, dry soil in full sun.

A special herb garden is wonderful if you have room, but you can grow herbs among other garden plants. Golden or silver thymes, the variegated sages, lacy-leaved chervil and feathery fennel and dill can match any decorative plant for beauty; neat plants like upright thymes, cushion-forming chives and curly leaved parsley make a great edging for borders.

Containers
Big pots of mixed herbs look and smell fantastic, and their major advantage is they can be moved around to just where you want them. Outside the kitchen door is a good place, urging whoever is cooking to make full use of them! Use potting compost with extra grit to fill the containers, and make sure there are plenty of drainage holes in the base.

Regional recipe pots
Try planting up pots with the ingredients from a particular country, or for a specific kind of recipe.
Italian – plum tomatoes, basil, chard, sweet peppers and flat-leafed parsley.
Greek – aubergines, tomatoes and basil.
Indian – chillies, tomatoes and coriander.
French – tarragon, peppers and tomatoes.

Top 10 herbs
Basil: a tender annual available in a variety of sweet, spicy flavours.
Chives: lightly onion-flavoured spiky leaves and edible purple flowerheads.
Fennel: threadlike, anise-scented leaves on a tall, statuesque plant.
Mint: best in containers to curb its invasive ways; apple mint is very fragrant.
Parsley: flat-leaved varieties are best for flavour, curly leaved ones for looks.
Rosemary: a perennial shrub with narrow, silvery leaves and delicate blue flowers.
Sage: attractive perennial shrub with aromatic, wrinkled, grey-green leaves.
Savory: perennial winter savory and annual summer savory have aromatic leaves that go well with green beans.
Tarragon: seek out the finer-flavoured French tarragon rather than the Russian.
Thyme: tiny, aromatic leaves in a wide range of decorative varieties.

Opposite: A garden devoted to herbs is lovely if you have the space, but herbs can be grown in amongst other ornamental plants to great effect, as these gardens demonstrate. Variegated-leaved varieties are particularly effective, and many herbs have decorative flowers, too.

APRIL

"If March proceeds at a trot, when April takes over she canters along. Decisions need to be finalised about what and where and when. Practising rotation is important, and though it may be a counsel of perfection should your plot be tiny, it is still worth trying to implement it. And the benefits will soon become clear. It's an age-old pratice that allows soil fertility to be maintained. At no time more than in April is the primacy of the soil more obvious. Now, the riches of the compost heap can be appreciated as the rich dark treasure is incorporated into the warming soil. Some people feed the plants but good gardeners feed the soil. It has a lot of work to do and it needs all the help we can give it. As well as the extra warmth, there will be rain too and this is the time to work out a strategy for conserving water.

As crops emerge, use leaf mould and compost as a mulch to conserve moisture and keep down weeds. It is always best to sow small amounts successively and far more interesting to try different varieties of veg. The cardinal rule though, is to grow lots of what you love to eat. After all, these are vegetables and this is food; it's for eating…

On warm days, you can feel the sun on the back of your neck and almost hear the crops growing. There may be setbacks, cold snaps and dreary days but the vegetables are on the march and nothing is going to stop them.

Jobs for April

Sow for succession Once the first sowings are a few centimetres tall, it is time, in many cases, to make further sowings to get a continuous supply of crops. Peas crop for about two weeks in summer; to cover the whole period, you can sow up to four times in spring for a regular supply. Since salad crops become unappetizing very quickly, sow seed little and often.

Water where necessary With the soil still moist from winter, you seldom need to water in spring, but cold dry winds can parch seedbeds, so light watering is helpful.

Thin seedlings As soon as seedlings can be handled, start thinning them out where they are too thick. Where appropriate, transplant some of the seedlings to fill gaps.

Resow poor results Failures will occur, particularly from early sowings, when the weather might not have been ideal. If this happens, sow again with fresh seed. This is why you should always hold some seed in reserve.

Continue sowing transplants Brussels sprouts, leeks, summer cabbages and cauliflowers can continue to be sown indoors or in an outdoor seedbed for transplanting to their final positions later on.

Harden off indoor-raised plants Seedlings sown earlier under cover must be gradually accustomed to cooler conditions before they are planted in their final positions.

Buy in plants If you have not raised your own plants, garden centres are usually well stocked with small pots of tender and hardy crops. The best ones sell quickly, and those that don't soon deteriorate under garden centre conditions. Buy as soon as possible even if you have to keep them under fleece or on a sunny windowsill until you are ready to plant.

Earth up potatoes As soon as the first shoots emerge from the earliest-planted potatoes, draw soil right over the tops to protect them from frost. Continue to do this until all danger of frost has passed. If a particularly hard frost is forecast, cover the shoots with straw or newspaper as well, for an extra layer of protection.

Keep things tidy Vegetable plots should look good, so keep weeding and tidying edges and paths, and removing debris. Tidiness helps prevent accidents in the garden (leaving less around for you to lose or trip over), and deprives slugs and other pests of shelter.

Week 1

> **Home-grown vegetables only have to travel from the plot to the table – food inches rather than food miles**

Spinach

So many people have strong feelings about spinach. You love it or hate it – and I love it. Spinach leaves are among the very best raw in salads, and if they're allowed to grow larger, they're delicious lightly cooked.

Spinach tips
• Don't attempt to grow spinach in poor, dry soil – it needs plenty of moisture and nutrients. Apply a general fertilizer and add plenty of well-rotted manure or compost to the soil before sowing.
• To grow small, tender salad leaves, make a wide drill and scatter the seed thinly across it. The seedlings will not need thinning.
• Spinach will not germinate well in hot weather, and tends to bolt if sown too early. Sow from mid-spring to early summer for summer leaves, and again in autumn for a winter supply.

Recommended varieties
'Scenic' AGM: High-yielding with large, bright green leaves; particularly suitable as a cut-and-come again crop. Resistant to mildew.
'Toscane' AGM: Late-maturing with smooth, good-looking leaves and high yields. Slow to bolt.
'Bordeaux': Very attractive, dark green leaves with contrasting red leaf veins and stems make this a good baby spinach for salads.
'Medania' AGM: Bulks up reliably with slightly blistered, large round leaves. Slow to bolt even in hot weather.

Week 2

Spinach roulade

On our market stall many years ago we used to sell our surplus spinach with a big **Popeye** label to advertise it, and it sold out almost as soon as we got there. Spinach is full of fibre and minerals but remember, it does cook down to almost nothing, so you need plenty of leaves.

Ingredients

Serves 4

50g (2oz) butter, softened
375g (12oz) fresh spinach, washed and
    cooked until tender
3 eggs, separated
salt and pepper

FILLING
375g (12oz) cream cheese
1 bunch spring onions, chopped
175g (6oz) broccoli, trimmed,
    blanched, and finely chopped
4 tomatoes, skinned, deseeded
    and finely chopped

Method

Preheat the oven to 190°C/375°F/gas mark 5. Line a 23 x 30cm (9 x 12in) Swiss roll tin with greaseproof paper and brush lightly with some of the butter. Squeeze all the liquid from the cooked spinach; chop finely or purée. Beat in the remaining butter, the egg yolks and salt and pepper to taste. Whisk the egg whites until just stiff, then fold into the spinach mixture. Turn into the prepared tin and cook in the oven for 10–15 minutes.

To make the filling, beat the cream cheese and spring onions together. Mix the broccoli and tomatoes into the cream cheese and season well.

Turn the cooked roulade out on to clean greaseproof paper. Carefully peel off the lining paper and trim the edges. Spread the filling evenly over three-quarters of the roulade and roll up from the unfilled end. Wrap paper tightly over the roulade and chill for 30 minutes, before serving sliced, with a few salad leaves.

Week 3

> **Gardening provides an opportunity to re-establish a relationship with the soil**

Sowing outside

Above: Sow seed thinly in a shallow drill and cover it lightly with soil.

Soil temperatures of at least 6°C (43°F) are needed for most seed to germinate, and this is reached by mid-spring in most of England, two weeks later in colder districts and two weeks earlier in mild regions.

Seed must be buried in the soil, but not so deeply that it cannot emerge, and not so shallowly that it dries out. You need a seedbed in which the previously cultivated soil is raked level to create a smooth layer of finely divided soil over firm, but not too hard, underlying soil. This can be done only if the soil is dry. Spread a light dressing of an all-purpose fertilizer on the soil before raking.

Make a groove, called a drill, in the surface just deep enough to cover the seed to about twice its diameter or, in the case of small seed, as shallow as possible but still enough to cover.

The groove can be made using the corner of a hoe or rake or by using the length of a broom handle pressed into the soil. Water the drill and sow the seed in it in a sparse, continuous flow, with about 1cm (½in) between each seed. Alternatively, sow five or six seeds wherever you want a plant (e.g. lettuces or turnips), later thinning to one plant. Draw back the soil to fill the drill.

The seed and soil must be in close contact if the seed is to take up moisture from the ground. The easiest way to make sure this happens is to firm down the soil by pressing on it with the head of the rake. Do it firmly if the soil is dry, and lightly if it's moist. Some soils pack down under rain so solidly that the seed cannot emerge; if this is a danger in your veg plot, cover the seed instead with fine potting compost.

What to sow

By the end of April, the more tender crops such as courgettes, dwarf French beans, and sweetcorn may be sown outside in mild areas, but timing does vary according to where you garden – in colder regions, you may need to hang on a little longer. If there is a risk of frost once the seeds have germinated, cover them with fleece or cloches. Other crops like beetroot, carrot, cabbage, kohl rabi, leek, lettuce, parsley, parsnip, pea, salad onion, spinach, sprouting broccoli, swede and turnips can be sown freely.

Week 4

From seeds to young plants

Above: Seedlings will usually need to be thinned to their optimum spacing.

Different seeds take different lengths of time to germinate. Members of the cabbage family and lettuces may take just seven days, while slow-germinating seed like onions and carrots take, on average, 14–21 days to emerge. Most other seed takes somewhere in between. Soil temperatures also have an effect on germination times, with low temperatures slowing things down.

Seedlings

Small seed makes small seedlings, and these take a long time to put on good growth (carrots and onions are good examples) whereas large seed (e.g. peas and broad beans) produce large seedlings that get off to a flying start.

Seedlings are vulnerable to fungal diseases such as damping off, but sowing at the optimum time, when the soil is warm and not too wet, greatly reduces

the risk. Watering seedlings raised indoors with copper-based fungicides also protects them. However, disease can often be avoided altogether by using clean containers and clean water.

Seedlings sown directly in the soil outdoors will need to be protected from pests, diseases and the weather, and you must prevent weeds competing with them for space and food.

Thinning

Seedlings can be left to grow where they germinate, although they usually need to be thinned to their final spacing by removing the weakest ones. They can also be 'gapped up' by sowing more seed or moving surplus seedlings to fill any gaps, though root crops like carrots and parsnips don't like to be moved.

Pricking out

Seeds sown in trays indoors are likely to need moving to wider spacing, either in similar size trays or in individual pots or modules, before they are ready to be planted outside. Move the seedlings as soon as they can be handled, and handle them by their seed leaves (the large leaves that appear first), never by their stems. Use a small dibber to lever them out of the compost and replant them.

Feeding your seedlings

Start liquid feeding after about six weeks, or as soon as the lower leaves go yellow. Peat-free composts will need more feeding and watering. Use any general-purpose liquid fertilizer.

Right: Seedlings raised in modules can be planted out with minimum root disturbance.

Providing support

Not all vegetables need supports, but those that grow tall, carry a heavy crop, or are in exposed, windy positions, will certainly benefit. There are various types of supports and stakes that can be used.

Canes and poles

These are good for tall, scrambling plants like runner beans. One popular way to use them is to set about six or eight canes in a circle, and tie the tips firmly together to form a wigwam. Sow or plant a bean at the base of each cane. If you are growing a larger number of plants, set the canes in a double row and tie each pair of opposite canes together at the top, giving extra support to the structure by laying more canes horizontally along the ridge and tying these in place. Bean poles are branches or stems of young trees and are thicker and sturdier than canes, but can be used in much the same way.

Canes are also useful for supporting bushy plants such as tomatoes and peppers, which tend to flop if left to their own devices, particularly when laden with fruit. Supply one to three canes per plant and tie the plants with twine in a figure-of-eight loop.

Pea sticks

Twiggy sticks are perfect supports for plants such as peas which need just a little help to keep them upright. Cut twiggy, branching stems of hazel or similar bushes in the winter, while the stems are bare, making them 1–1.2m

Left: Wigwams of canes make a decorative support for climbing beans.

Above: Sturdy supports will be necessary to carry the weight of plants in full crop.

(3–4ft) long. Push the bases of the pea sticks into the soil close to the pea seedlings. As the peas grow, their tendrils will twine among the twiggy stems to hold up the plants. Smaller versions can be used for lower growing plants.

Netting

Plastic netting stretched between canes or poles can be used to support climbing and scrambling plants like beans and peas. Be sure there are plenty of upright supports, as the netting becomes very heavy when covered by the plants.

Stakes

In exposed gardens, a sturdy stake will prevent tall winter brassicas such as Brussels sprouts being blown over in bad weather. In windy areas, a sturdy stake may be a better proposition than canes for plants like tomatoes, too.

Discouraging pests

Late spring and early summer is when plant pests really start to make their presence felt. You can't miss the likes of snails and slugs, caterpillars and rabbits; but other pests, such as red spider mite, are barely visible.

Helping plants to fight

Instead of waging war directly on pests and diseases, vegetable growers should boost natural counter-measures and avoid harming helpful organisms.
• Well-grown plants with sufficient water and nutrients fend off insect attacks much more readily than stressed plants.
• Make life inhospitable for the pests, removing hiding places and limiting access by clearing debris and weeds.
• Prevent pests reaching the crop with barriers. Carrot fly and cabbage root fly can be excluded with fleece or insect-proof mesh. Surround carrot crops with a 50cm (20in) high barrier of plastic sheeting to keep carrot fly at bay, and counter cabbage root fly by putting a felt collar round the base of the plant.

Pesticides

The final remedy is to apply an insecticide or other chemical, but this should seldom be necessary. So-called directed sprays with a physical action (such as oils, soaps and fatty acids) will do least harm to helpful insects. Of those that poison insects, the natural ones, such as pyrethrum, are short-lived and mild.

Dealing with slugs and snails

The first step is to keep the garden tidy and eliminate hiding places. Aluminium sulphate powder and ferric phosphate pellets are compatible with organic gardening; other more traditional remedies like beer traps and half-grapefruit skins are worth trying to reduce pest numbers. Biological control with nematodes (microscopic, wormlike animals) is effective in summer, but affects only certain slugs.

Top left: Keep plants well watered and fed to help them fend off pest attacks.

Top right: Regular weeding and tidying around crops removes hiding places for pests.

Bottom left: Beer traps provide one way of keeping slug and snail numbers under control.

Bottom right: Felt collars will prevent cabbage root flies laying eggs near the roots of brassicas.

CAROL'S GREEN TIP

PEST-RESISTANT VARIETIES

Some vegetable varieties have an inbuilt resistance to pests and diseases, and are less likely to be badly affected by them. Examples include carrots 'Flyaway' and 'Resistafly', which are resistant to carrot root fly; clubroot-resistant cauliflower 'Clapton'; and courgette 'Defender', which is resistant to mosaic virus. Growing resistant varieties means you are more likely to be able to avoid using chemical pesticides and fungicides.

MAY

" Always the best month in the garden, May is full of froth and freshness. Hand-in-hand with the rest of the garden, the vegetable plot greens up. Almost imperceptibly, salads, spinach, beetroot and chard make patterns of purple and every shade of green and the brown earth begins to disappear under their burgeoning advance.

Hopefully the bulk of our sowing is done, but there are always omissions, mistakes and minor disasters, at least there are in my garden. May offers the opportunity to rectify them all. It is a kindly month, the soil is auspiciously warm and there is often gentle rain, perfect sowing conditions for successional sowing or starting again. Seed germinates rapidly and rows and blocks already sown in March and April have melded together to create a tapestry. There is an opportunity to see where there are gaps that can be filled either with fresh sowings or some of the baby plants you so cunningly started earlier.

By the middle of the month we have said goodbye to frosts, and tender crops can be introduced to the big wide world. The whole cucurbit family appeals to me, they are up-front plants and though they are all frost-tender, once they are planted out in rich soil with the sun shining on them and getting warmer every day, nothing can halt their progress. Such lust for life is always an encouragement, especially following a cold, slow spring. Best of all is harvesting. Suddenly there are enough leaves to fill a salad bowl, there may be young asparagus shoots to cut and the first baby beetroots and carrots to pull and you are once again reminded of the real motivation for growing your own – the taste. "

Jobs for May

Keep sowing By late spring, the main sowing season for hardy vegetables is over, except where planting successive sowings for a continuous supply. However, there are still important crops to come. Beetroot, late peas, carrots, calabrese, lettuces, onions, parsnips, radishes, rocket, swede, spring onions, turnips and spinach can be sown in the ground where they are to grow.

Raise transplants Sow seed, including cabbages and cauliflowers for autumn, spring and winter, and purple sprouting broccoli, in pots or cell trays under glass or a seedbed outdoors.

Sow frost-sensitive crops Sow French beans, courgettes, cucumbers, marrows, melons, pumpkins, squash and sweetcorn under glass. All have large seeds, which produce fast-growing plants, so sow only when the date of the last frost is no more than six weeks away.

Harden off early sowings Many of the transplants sown earlier in spring will be ready to go outdoors after hardening off. Brussels sprouts, salads, summer calabrese, cauliflowers and cabbages in particular appreciate early planting out.

Plant greenhouse crops Tender crops, such as aubergines, peppers and tomatoes, can be planted in greenhouse borders or growing bags. Those for growing outside need a few more weeks under glass before being moved out.

Catch up There is still time to sow and plant any crops that should have been raised earlier in spring; they invariably catch up. In fact, with badly drained gardens in cold exposed sites it is worth waiting until late spring.

Protect against pests By now, crops should be pushing up well. Since carrots, parsnips and cabbage-related crops are still vulnerable to pests, keep them covered with fleece or insect-proof nets for as long as possible.

Provide support Peas need sticks or mesh to climb up, and broad beans may need support from stakes and string.

Earth up potatoes Continue earthing up as shoots emerge to prevent the tubers from turning green. Draw soil up round the stems – you don't need to completely cover the shoots once the risk of frost is over.

Keep weeding Weed growth is at its peak. Hoeing on dry days reduces hand weeding to a minimum.

Thin seedlings Crops can be growing very fast, so thinning is a priority.

Outdoor sowing Courgettes, French beans, cucumbers, marrows, pumpkins, runner beans, squashes and sweetcorn can be sown outdoors in sheltered, mild districts, where they are to grow. They will develop superior roots systems that help them grow fast.

Week 1

Broad Beans

Broad beans are beans for beginners – anyone can grow them. They make strong, handsome plants with their blue-grey foliage and dense clusters of sweetly scented flowers.

Broad bean tips
• For the earliest crop, sow outdoors in autumn while the soil is still warm. Choose a sheltered position and a hardy variety. Otherwise, sow seed outside from early spring onwards, aiming for a series of small successional sowings of 8–12 seeds.
• Mature plants are liable to wind damage, so they need a sunny, sheltered site. Strong, twiggy prunings create an unobtrusive network of support.

• When the young beans begin to appear at the base of the plant, pinch out the growing tips to concentrate the plants' energy on pod formation, nipping off the top of the stem with two pairs of leaves attached. These leafy tips are delicious when lightly cooked.
• If black bean aphids are colonizing the young shoots, pinch them out with the tips of your finger and thumb.

Recommended varieties
'The Sutton' AGM: Dwarf variety, excellent for exposed sites and small gardens. A prolific cropper.
'Aquadulce Claudia' AGM: Suitable for sowing outdoors in warm soil in autumn. Hardy and early maturing.

Week 2

> **Podding broad beans is a sensual delight, the hard, shiny exterior contrasting with the furry interiors that enclose the beans**

Hot asparagus with balsamic vinegar

Asparagus is the perfect vegetable to grow at home – it's a real gourmet treat that is incredibly expensive in the shops. An established asparagus bed can last for up to 20 years, giving you armfuls of tender, tasty spears. Enjoy it simply cooked to make the most of its short, early summer season.

Ingredients

Serves 4

500g (1lb) young asparagus spears, trimmed
50g (2oz) pine nuts, toasted
25g (1oz) Parmesan cheese, shaved into slivers
salt and pepper

BALSAMIC VINEGAR DRESSING
2 tablespoons balsamic vinegar
1–2 garlic cloves, crushed
375g (12oz) tomatoes, skinned, deseeded and finely chopped
5 tablespoons olive oil

Method

To make the dressing, mix the balsamic vinegar, garlic, tomatoes and olive oil in a bowl and set aside.

Heat a griddle pan, add the asparagus in a single layer and cook for 5 minutes over a medium heat, turning constantly.

Divide the asparagus between four warmed plates. Spoon over the balsamic vinegar dressing, top with the pine nuts and Parmesan shavings. Season with salt and pepper and serve at once.

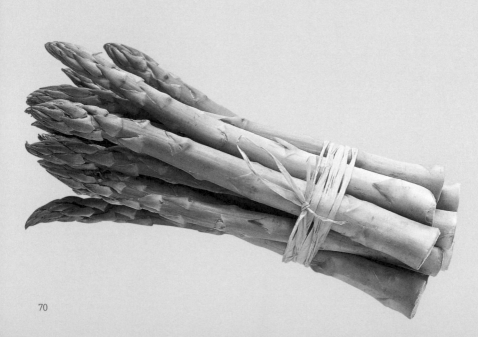

Week **3**

Late spring sowings

Above left: Most brassicas can be sown in a prepared seedbed for subsequent transplanting to their final positions.

Above right: Make successional sowings of French beans to extend their cropping period.

There are still plenty of sowings to be made outside in the garden now. As conditions get warmer, most seeds will germinate more rapidly, but you will need to start watering newly sown seeds and emerging seedlings if the weather turns dry.

Plants that do not like cold conditions can all safely be sown outside now. French beans can continue to be sown into next month for successional cropping, but runner beans, swede and sweetcorn should be sown as early as it is safe to do so in order to give the plants the longest possible growing season. Carry on making successional sowings of crops like beetroot, carrots, peas, radish, spinach and turnips.

Sowing in a seedbed

Plants of the cabbage family intended for harvesting in winter can be sown now. They are usually sown outdoors in a seedbed and transplanted to their final positions later.

It is virtually impossible to avoid damaging roots when transplanting plants. To minimize this, prepare the seedbed thoroughly, and add well-rotted garden or bagged compost to lighten the texture of the soil, making it easier to lift the plants. Sow seed thinly, so that the seedlings do not become overcrowded.

Brassicas that can be sown in a seedbed now include sprouting broccoli, cauliflower, kale and autumn and winter cabbages. Calabrese, or green heading broccoli, is one crop that is better sown direct rather than transplanted from a seedbed. It is very sensitive to any disturbance to its growth, which can result in the production of premature 'button' heads.

Week **4**

> **Don't worry if you have room only for assorted pots, tubs and window boxes – you can still grow a good range of produce**

Growing in containers

If you are not lucky enough to have room for a vegetable plot, all is not lost. Containers arranged in groups near the kitchen make an attractive feature, and you can get surprisingly good yields.

Types of container

Containers in a huge range of shapes and materials are now readily available. Ensure that the pot size is appropriate for what you want to grow: root vegetables such as carrots need deep pots, while beetroot sits near to the top of the soil so needs less depth. Shallower pots are also fine for salads. Big plants such as tomatoes and courgettes need large pots to accommodate their roots. For tall plants that need a stable base, use a heavy pot and fill with soil-based compost.

Drainage

Good drainage is important; check that there are enough drainage holes in the base of the container, and if not, make some more. Cover the base of the pot with old crocks or stones and raise the pots on feet to help water drain through.

Watering

Potting compost needs to be moist at all times. Do not rely on rainfall because it may not penetrate the leaf cover of the plants, or be heavy enough to soak down to the roots. Mix non-organic water-retaining gel or powder in with the compost when planting. The gel swells when wetted, and then releases water gradually back into the compost. Mulching the surface with gravel or organic materials helps minimize evaporation. If you have many pots, it might be worth installing an automatic irrigation system.

Potting compost

Use either a water-retentive peat- or bark-based potting compost, or a soil- or loam-based medium (such as John Innes potting compost) for your vegetables. Most types of multi-purpose potting composts are also suitable.

Feeding

The relatively small amount of compost in a pot will have limited nutrients for plants. Incorporating a controlled-release fertilizer on planting will help; otherwise use a general-purpose feed.

Crops and varieties to grow

Beetroot, carrots, courgettes, cucumber, French beans, peppers, herbs, radish, potatoes, tomatoes, lettuce and peppers can all be grown in pots. Look for compact varieties – for instance, bush varieties of courgettes, short-rooted carrots and baby beet. Many seed catalogues include vegetables specially bred for small spaces, such as tomato 'Tumbling Tom' for hanging baskets.

Top left: Containers are very useful for starting seeds, but many crops can also be grown to maturity in pots.

Top right: There are plenty of unusual containers to add extra interest to your garden.

Bottom: Container-grown vegetables are ideal for patio gardens where space is limited.

Late spring shortcuts

Raising your own plants from seed is always rewarding, but sometimes it's not possible, or practical. You need a fair amount of space early in the season; if you have a large heated greenhouse you're fine, but if you're limited to balancing seed trays and pots on windowsills in the home or in a tiny porch you will be pushed for space to grow everything you want.

If you need only a small number of plants, such as half-a-dozen tomatoes, or a couple of courgettes or sweet peppers, it's not usually economical to go to the trouble of raising a trayful of seedlings, only to end up giving most of them away or putting them on the compost heap.

Top: Any good garden centre will have a wide selection of young, container-grown herbs and vegetable plants in spring.

Bottom left: Broad beans grown in modules can be planted with the minimum of root disturbance.

Bottom right: Harden plants off before setting them out in their final growing positions outside.

Then, of course, there are the odd disasters we all have, when a batch of seedlings fails to grow, or perhaps succumbs to damping-off disease. In all these instances, it can be much more convenient to buy in young, healthy plants which someone else has had the trouble of raising.

Plug plants

More and more vegetable plants are available at this time of year as plug plants – young plants growing in small, individual plugs of compost, all ready to plant out. A good selection is available from the catalogues of mail order seed companies, though these normally have to be ordered before mid-spring. Good garden centres should have plenty in stock now, though. Make sure your young plants come from a reputable source; surplus plants offered to you by a neighbour are tempting, but if they introduce diseases such as club root to your garden you will curse the day you accepted. Plants should have been raised in sterile seed compost to avoid this.

CHOOSING THE BEST PLANTS

Look for plants:
- with healthy, rich green leaves and a strong, undamaged growing point
- with good root growth, with space for further root development
- that have been well cared for

Don't buy plants:
- that are overlarge and where the compost has been allowed to dry out
- that have very tightly packed roots
- with any signs of pests or diseases.

Growing for showing

Entering your best vegetables at a local show is great fun. Even if you don't win a prize, you will no doubt enjoy the experience, and chatting to the other exhibitors is a chance for you to learn a lot.

Gardening clubs and allotment societies will usually be able to tell you about your local shows. The most important document to get hold of is the show schedule: this tells you exactly what produce is eligible for entry and how it must be displayed on show day. If you don't follow the rules exactly, the judges will mark your exhibit 'NAS' (not according to schedule), disqualifying it.

Biggest is not always best when it comes to showing; it is more important that your vegetables are in prime condition and grown to perfection. Browse through lots of seed catalogues over the winter; you will find some varieties are specially recommended for showing.

You will need to prepare the soil thoroughly, grow the right varieties, start the plants at the right time to give them a good long growing season, and feed and water them to keep them growing without a check. You will also need to protect your plants from weather or accidental damage, and from pests and diseases.

You will find some growers take showing very seriously and have all sorts of special equipment and techniques to help them produce prize-winning veg. If you come up against such specialists at your local show, you will find it hard to beat them, but you can marvel at their perfect exhibits while consoling yourself that at least yours will taste just as good, if not better!

Show tips
• Make sure crops like beans, cucumbers and marrows have room to hang down so that they can grow perfectly straight. Do not allow the skins of marrow and cucumbers to become scratched or marked.
• For root crops such as carrots and parsnips, dig the soil very deeply. Some growers make deep holes with a crowbar and then fill them with sifted soil to ensure the roots can grow long and straight.
• Read the schedule carefully to make sure your exhibit complies.
• Where more than one item is required in an exhibit (for instance, five runner beans), these should be as perfectly matched as possible.
• Pick your exhibits on the morning of the show if possible, so they are completely fresh. Handle them as little as you can.
• Display your exhibit attractively. Go round a few shows before you take the plunge, to see how it's done.

Top: The cultivation of show-stopping leeks and other vegetables is a serious business for many specialist growers.

Bottom: Blemishes on the skin of this pumpkin may reduce its potential as a top prizewinner.

JUNE

" Heading for the longest day, there is a feeling of optimism, warmth and a sense of upsurge. Plants, plants and more plants – to sow, plant out, pot on, feed, mulch and nourish. June is the nurturing month when every crop is crying out for attention. An observant eye and an empathetic response now to thinning, weeding and transplanting will pay manifold dividends further down the line.

June can have sudden hot spots and watering takes on a new priority. Having enough to drink is vitally important, especially for newly emerging seedlings and transplanted crops. Since water is such a precious resource, it is always worth spending extra time making sure it is used where it is most valuable – on the roots. It is a leisurely activity too and enables us to keep a close eye on how things are going, it keeps us in touch with our plants.

Weeds and pests are suddenly apparent, the blackfly on the broad bean tips or the groundsel amongst the cabbages are easy to spot and take action on. Where crops are in rows, drawing a sharp hoe between them is both satisfying and efficient. Always try to do it when the sun is beating down to shrivel them up.

The routine of tying in wayward beans or sweet peas and dashing in with the twiggy sticks to give peas some extra support reinforces the feeling of growth and reminds us of the cycle where we all play our part. It's very satisfying to help plants do their best. Everyday there is more to harvest and enjoy. "

Jobs for June

Begin harvesting The first baby carrots, beetroot, broad beans, salads and peas are ready in early summer. Since their freshness declines with age, harvest immediately. This also frees the space for later crops.

Act early Long days, moist soil, warm temperatures and a high sun give excellent growth. By late summer, conditions are less favourable, so get all crops planted and growing by mid-June.

Keep planting As space becomes available, lightly cultivate the ground, add fertilizer, and sow or plant. All remaining hardy plants, including cabbages, cauliflowers, celery and leeks, should be planted out as soon as possible. Tender plants raised under glass can also be planted out after hardening off. A fleece covering helps to boost growth in cool districts. Aubergines, melons and peppers seldom thrive without extra protection outdoors.

Give plants support Make sure that plants are correctly tied in to their supports. Runner beans may need encouragement to start climbing up bamboo canes; wrap some rough twine round the base of the canes to give the shoots something to cling on to.

Sow sensitive crops By this time, crops that bolt if they encounter cold nights and/or short days can be sown. These include chicory, endive and oriental greens like Chinese cabbage. (See page 94 for more about 'bolting'.)

Continue feeding Greedy cabbage family plants, beetroot, celery, celeriac and leeks benefit from supplementary feeding, and container-grown vegetables need regular liquid feed throughout the growing season.

Make an extra sowing In warm districts, it is worth sowing crops like French beans, runner beans, and courgettes in cell trays to plant out as space becomes free in late summer.

Earth up potatoes These can be given their final earthing up.

Continue weeding Deal with weeds as soon as they emerge, by hoeing or hand-weeding.

Watch out for pests Insect pests, including blackfly, caterpillars, greenfly and leaf mining insects, begin to cause damage in summer. Red spider mite thrives in hot, dry conditions, causing leaf loss on French beans, runner beans and crops under glass. If damage threatens to become significant, act promptly.

Ward off disease In dry seasons, powdery mildew can be damaging to courgettes, cucumbers, peas, pumpkins and swedes. Careful watering to keep the soil moist can limit damage.

Finish planting greenhouse crops Crops such as tomatoes, peppers, aubergines and cucumbers to be grown to maturity under cover should be planted as soon as possible now.

Week 1

Carrots

Choose the right varieties and you can harvest carrots from mid-May to March. They store well over winter and come in a range of shapes and colours – from red to purple.

Carrot tips

• To grow long-rooted carrots, you need a good loam or sandy soil that can be deeply cultivated. If your soil is shallow, stony or heavy clay, then opt for stump-rooted or round varieties.

• For an early crop to harvest from late spring, sow in late winter in a cold frame or under cloches.

• Sow carrots sparingly to avoid the need for thinning later on – the scent of the crushed foliage attracts carrot root fly. When thinning is necessary, do it in the evening to reduce the smell from the leaves. Space about 5cm (2in) apart.

• Deter carrot roof fly further by netting crops or by covering with fleece.

• Tender baby carrots are ready for harvesting about 12–16 weeks after sowing. Pull up young carrots by hand, while larger ones and those for storage are best lifted by easing up with a fork.

Recommended varieties

'Adelaide' AGM: Excellent early crop, suitable for sowing in frames.
'Flyaway': A medium-length maincrop with stump-ended roots and sweet flesh. Good resistance to carrot fly.
'Parmex' AGM: A round-rooted carrot, ideal for shallow soils and containers. Good uniformity and core colour.

Week **2**

> **Pull your carrots young, rinse them quickly and eat them raw**

Pea, lettuce and lemon soup

The excitement of holding a fat green pea pod between thumb and forefinger and popping it open is magical – gardening doesn't get much better. Here peas combine with lettuce to form a refreshing soup that is ideal for a summer lunch. Lettuce might seem an unusual in a soup, but it's surprisingly good cooked.

Ingredients

Serves 4

25g (1oz) butter
1 large onion, finely chopped
425g (14oz) peas
2 'Little Gem' or similar lettuces, roughly chopped
1 litre (1¾ pints) vegetable stock
grated rind and juice of ½ lemon
salt and pepper

SESAME CROÛTONS
2 thick slices of bread, cut into cubes
1 tablespoon olive oil
1 tablespoon sesame seeds

Method

Preheat the oven to 200°C/400°F/Gas mark 6. To make the croûtons, brush the bread cubes with the oil and spread out in a roasting tin. Sprinkle with the sesame seeds and bake in the oven for 10–15 minutes, until golden.

Meanwhile, melt the butter in a large, heavy-based saucepan, add the onion and cook over a moderate heat for 5 minutes or until softened. Add the peas, lettuce, stock, lemon rind and juice and salt and pepper to taste. Bring to the boil, then reduce the heat, cover and simmer for 10–15 minutes.

In a blender or food processor, blend the soup in batches until smooth, then return it to the pan. Taste and adjust the seasoning if necessary. Reheat gently. Ladle into warm soup bowls and serve sprinkled with the sesame croûtons.

Week 3

Early summer feeding

Above: Nitrogen-rich fertilizers are ideal to boost the growth of leafy brassica crops.

If you have prepared your soil well, it should contain good reserves of nutrients. However, greedy crops, such as brassicas, often need the boost of supplementary feeding. Light, free-draining soils tend to run short of soluble nutrients quickly as they are easily washed away.

Fertilizers contain the nutrients nitrogen (N), phosphorus (P) and potassium (K) in varying proportions. Nitrogen-rich fertilizers encourage leafy growth, so are good for leaf crops like spinach and chard. Phosphorus-rich fertilizers encourage root growth, so are good for root crops. Potassium (or potash)-rich fertilizers encourage fruit and flower formation and are good for fruiting crops such as tomatoes and courgettes.

Measuring the nutrients

Fertilizer packs display the percentages they contain of nitrogen, phosphorus and potassium (N:P:K, in that order). You will need to use three times as much fertilizer containing 7% nitrogen as one containing 21% nitrogen, but always follow the instructions on the pack.

Organic fertilizers

Organic fertilizers are composed of naturally occurring sources of nutrients, such as dried blood, bonemeal, hoof and horn, fish and bone, and poultry manure. However, some organic fertilizers are products of intensive farming systems or slaughterhouses and many people may object to using them.

CAROL'S GREEN TIP

GO EASY ON THE FERTILIZER

Using too much fertilizer can lead to big problems for the environment. Nitrogen is very soluble, and is easily washed out of the soil into rivers, where it causes the rapid growth of algae. This upsets the balance of river life and can kill fish and other wildlife. Use fertilizers only when they are needed, apply at the proper time and stick to recommended application rates.

Week 4

> One of the greatest joys of harvesting your own crops is to feel part of the real, natural world around you

Watering your garden

We always hope for hot, sunny weather at this time of year, but without rain, plants will soon start to wilt as their water supply runs out. Windy conditions are almost as bad as heat and sun for drawing moisture away from plants, so if a lack of rain is coupled with a breezy spell, plants can be in trouble very quickly.

We have to learn to use water as efficiently as possible, and watering at the wrong time can be a complete waste. Luckily, we can benefit from lots of research that has been carried out into the optimum periods for watering vegetables.

Leafy crops such as cabbage, spinach and lettuce benefit from plentiful water supplies at every stage of growth, but the maximum response is gained by watering between seven and 14 days before you expect to harvest. Always water newly transplanted crops such as cabbages for several days after planting while their roots recover.

Root crops like beetroot, carrot and parsnip don't usually need watering unless it is so dry that their growth will be checked otherwise. Potatoes give higher yields when kept moist throughout, but particularly once the tubers have reached the size of marbles.

Fruiting and seeding crops such as tomatoes, peas and beans and sweetcorn should be watered when flowering starts (this helps fruits to set) and while the fruits or pods are swelling. Watering before flowering can increase leafy growth at the expense of the crop, and should be avoided.

Even outside these optimum times, you should never let any crop get so dry that it starts to wilt. A sudden deluge of moisture after a long dry spell can also cause fruits and roots to split. However, don't water little and often because this encourages shallow rooting – water thoroughly to soak the soil right down through the rooting zone.

Water conservation tips
• Water in the evening or at night, when evaporation is lowest.
• Avoid letting the soil dry out too much before watering.
• Direct water to the roots of plants rather than watering over a wide area; a seep or drip hose is particularly good at getting water where it's needed.
• Store rainwater and 'grey' household water (from baths, etc) in water butts.
• Mulch the soil surface round plants to reduce water loss by evaporation.
•Add plenty of organic matter to the soil to improve its water-holding capacity.
• Dig deeply to allow plant roots to penetrate into the soil's water reserves.

Top: A rose on a watering can breaks water up in small droplets, avoiding disturbance to young plants and soil.

Bottom left: Water courgettes once flowering starts: it will help the fruits to set and encourage them to swell.

Bottom right: Preserve water by storing rain in water butts.

Cut-and-come-again salads

There are scores of tasty, colourful and intriguingly textured salad plants that can be grown quickly from seed and cut as baby leaves. A few years ago, a standard salad might have been limp lettuce leaves, a few slices of soggy tomato and a radish – distinctly unappetizing. How all that has changed! And, of course, eating fresh leaves full of vitamins and minerals is the best possible diet.

Some old-fashioned lettuces, like 'Cos' and 'Webbs Wonderful', have a wonderful crunchy taste, but have to be picked whole when they are ready. Cut-and-come-again lettuce varieties such as 'Salad Bowl' and 'Oak Leaf' have taken over, offering delicious leaves for picking over a period of months. Two or three sowings should last a whole summer, taking you right into autumn.

And lettuce is just the start of it. There are a host of other salad leaves – chicory, endive, claytonia, sorrel, spinach, rocket – that can be used in this way.

Mesclun

One of the best salads is a good mesclun mix. A mesclun salad has no essential ingredients but is an elegant mixture of young leaves, according to what is available, always perfectly balanced so that no one ingredient dominates. Baby lettuce, rocket, lamb's lettuce, endive

and chervil are traditional; keeping to the spirit of mesclun, a modern mix might include other leaves such as Chinese and Japanese mustards, mizuna and mibuna. All are fast-growing and have various degrees of spicy heat.

Here are some of my favourite salad ingredients:

Buckler-leaved sorrel Bright green arrow-shaped leaves with a sharp lemony flavour.

Red orach Arrowhead-shaped leaves of deep maroon-red. Make a number of successional sowings because the young leaves are the most tender and have the best colour.

Corn salad (lamb's lettuce) Rosettes of small, bright green, succulent leaves. Very hardy, so a good source of salad over winter and in early spring, before it runs to seed. Sow in late summer or early autumn for a winter crop, and again in early spring for a second crop.

Rocket Young leaves have a distinctive peppery taste. Sow successionally from early spring until very late summer, and snip the leaves off with scissors when about 15cm (6in) high. In the height of summer, rocket will bolt rapidly, the leaves becoming tough and coarse.

Left: Growing a range of different lettuce varieties will add zing to your salads, making them both tastier and more appealing to the eye.

Planting late crops

It took me a while to manage to grow Florence fennel well. Because it is a Mediterranean crop, I tried sowing it early, on the premise that it must need a long season, but each time I tried it bolted to flower.

Bolting is an annoying habit of some vegetables – it occurs when they decide to skip most of their growing stage and rush ahead straight into flower in order to set seeds. This usually means a wasted crop – either the plants have not made a sufficient amount of growth to harvest, or the quality of the growth that has been made is ruined.

Eventually I learned the trick with fennel – not to sow or plant it until this time of year. Bolting needs a trigger to set it off, and that trigger is usually a serious check to the growth of the plants; most often a sudden cold spell when the young plants are vulnerable.

Crops that may bolt
Endive and chicory are two more candidates for late planting and sowing, and Chinese cabbages and Chinese greens are notorious for their readiness to bolt if sown too early. Root crops can also be affected; early-sown beetroot and turnips may run to flower prematurely. Bolt-resistant varieties that are much less sensitive to temperature are often available.

Bolting through heat
Spinach and lettuce can give us the same problem, but with an opposite cause – hot weather, dry conditions and long days combine to trigger premature flowering. In summer, sow in moist soil in partially shaded sites. Choose a spinach variety described as 'slow to bolt' for summer sowings; with lettuce, sow small amounts in succession so plants can be cut before they have a chance to flower.

Top left and right: The herb fennel is easy to grow, producing attractive umbels of flowers (left), but Florence fennel (right) with its swollen leaf bases, is altogether more tricky to produce.

Bottom: Chicory will run to seed if it is sown too early, but get the timing right and you can look forward to a good crop.

CAROL'S LATE-GROWING SPINACH
Because true spinach is difficult to grow in hot weather, we grow a lot of perpetual spinach and spinach beet at this time of year. Perpetual spinach is the easiest kind to grow and the most heat-tolerant, but Swiss chard has a more distinctive flavour. A summer sowing of either of these should keep you in leaves all winter long.

> The beginning of fruition time. July is all about dreams coming true, of quite literally harvesting the fruits (and vegetables) of your labour. As temperatures soar, familiar scents begin to reassert themselves, the first roaring-red flowers of runner beans with an unexpectedly sweet perfume, the pungent aroma as the side shoots of tomatoes are pinched out and the smell of water on hot earth or the greenhouse path.
>
> This is the month to indulge in the bounty but also to make sure that it continues. It may seem contrary to be thinking about the winter ahead, planting out the last of the brassicas, sprouts and purple sprouting broccoli, kale and cauliflowers, but once they are in with the last of the leeks, there is time to indulge in cornucopic courgettes, earthy new potatoes and freshly-shelled peas (they are lucky to reach the kitchen in our house). Not only can they be podded outside, sitting on the step in the sun, but on balmy evenings, they can be eaten there, too.
>
> Fresh tastes and aromas abound: herbs, especially 'dry' herbs, thyme, marjoram, sage and rosemary are particularly redolent and flavoursome harvested in the heat of the day. Those with soft leaves – mint, basil, parsley and coriander – need plenty of water and are best picked in the morning, full of sap and bedewed. It's time to experiment with new combinations, the chef's palette never has more colours and flavours: broad beans with beetroot, pea sprouts with baby carrots and sauce verte concocted with sorrel, spinach, cress and parsley or as you wander by, a handful of juicy leaves.

Jobs for July

Potatoes and tomatoes Blight is now a constant menace for potatoes and outdoor tomatoes, especially in wet seasons, when regular protective spraying is necessary.

Check on weeds Weed growth should slow down in summer, but survivors of earlier weeding sessions will need to be pulled out before they can set flower and scatter their seed.

Harvest The more you pick crops such as courgettes, beans and tomatoes, the more will be produced, so harvest frequently. If you let some fruits mature, the plant will think its job of seed production is done, and will cease cropping. Surplus produce can be frozen, made into pickles and chutneys, or offered to friends and neighbours.

Extra crops As soil becomes free, sow quick-growing crops of beetroot, French beans, kohl rabi, radishes, winter salad leaves and turnips.

Harvest salads Cut salad leaves while they are still young and tender. Make another sowing of mixed leaves in a sheltered place for a late cut.

Gather herbs for drying Pick leafy herbs such as parsley, tarragon, rosemary and thyme in the early morning of a warm, sunny day, once the dew has dried off the leaves. Hang them up in small loose bunches in a dim, airy place to dry.

Harvest early potatoes Brush some of the soil away from a potato plants to check on the size of the tubers; as soon as they are large enough to eat, you can start to enjoy them.

Greenhouse crops Greenhouse crops, such as tomatoes, cucumbers, peppers and melons need water and liquid feed, and also support. Use biological controls if pests like whitefly and red spider mite start to get out of hand.

Thin seedlings Vegetables sown for succession will need thinning to the appropriate spacing.

Sow lettuce and spinach Hot weather prevents lettuce seed from germinating and causes spinach seedlings to rush up to seed, so both these crops should be sown in a shady, moist place. Choose a suitable variety of spinach for summer sowing, such as 'Galaxy' or 'Giant Winter'.

Blanch leeks If you want a good length of white, blanched stem, pull a little soil up round the base of leeks now. Be careful not to get soil into the centres of the plants.

Water runner beans Beans need to have plenty of moisture at the roots all the time they are flowering, as this encourages the flowers to set.

Week 1

Beetroot

The humble beet is being increasingly valued as a tasty and unique ingredient in salads, soups and stews. And it's not just the roots that are mouth-watering – its bright green, purple-veined leaves, glistening with dressing, make a fine addition to a salad bowl.

Beetroot tips
• Each 'seed' is actually a fruit composed of three or four seeds. Thin the seedlings to leave just one per station, 10cm (4in) apart.
• From early spring to summer, sow a short row every couple of weeks for a regular supply of tender roots.
• Light, free-draining soil produces the best early crops. Heavier soils can be pre-warmed by putting cloches in place for several weeks before sowing.
• Water thoroughly every 10–14 days during dry spells. Lack of water causes woody roots while fluctuating water supplies can cause splitting.
• Tender baby beets can be harvested from golf-ball size. Don't let them get larger than a tennis-ball, however, or they may develop an unpleasant, woody texture.

Recommended varieties
'Pablo': An early variety with smooth skin and fine colour, free from internal rings. Good resistance to bolting.
'Boltardy': Recommended for early sowing, this is a smooth skinned, bolt-resistant variety with a fine colour.

Week 2

> There is nothing more rewarding than harvesting perfect, fresh vegetables and carrying them triumphantly back to the kitchen

Beetroot salad with coriander and tomato salsa

I prefer my beetroot small, and I always squeeze in little rows of beetroot here and there in the vegetable garden, sowing them perhaps every fortnight, so that I have a long succession of sweet little ruby-red beets to pull up.

Ingredients
Serves 4
8 small beetroots
2 tablespoons red wine vinegar
1 teaspoon caster sugar
2 tablespoons light olive oil
salt and pepper
crème fraîche, to serve
coriander sprigs, to garnish

SALSA
1 red onion, finely chopped
425g (14oz) small vine-ripened
   tomatoes, deseeded and chopped
2 garlic cloves, crushed
15g (½oz) coriander, chopped

Method
Cook the beetroot in lightly salted simmering water until tender (approximately 25 minutes) and then peel. Allow to cool and slice.

In a large bowl, whisk together the vinegar, sugar, oil and salt and pepper. Add the sliced beetroot and toss.

Make the salsa in a separate bowl. Mix together the onion, tomatoes, garlic and coriander. Season lightly with salt and pepper.

Arrange the beetroot slices on a serving plate and pile the salsa on to the beetroot. Top with spoonfuls of crème fraîche and spoon over any dressing left in the beetroot bowl. Serve garnished with coriander sprigs.

Week 3

Harvesting summer vegetables

Every day now there will be more and more to harvest from your vegetable plot. Picking just enough for your meal and eating it straight away is ideal, but it's not always convenient or possible to eat produce straight after picking.

As soon as vegetables are picked, they start to deteriorate. Water evaporates from their tissues and is not replaced, so they lose their crispness and wrinkle.

It's really important to keep picking crops like peas, beans and courgettes as soon as they are ready; if you leave them on the plant they will quickly become over-mature, and production will slow down or even stop completely.

Above: Spread harvested onions out and use any damaged specimens immediately.

Harvesting tips
• Harvest vegetables as soon they are in perfect condition for eating.
• Try to pick first thing in the morning.
• Spread harvested vegetables out in a thin layer; don't pile them up in a heap.
• Cool your harvest as soon as possible. Move picked vegetables into the shade, and dunk or spray them with cold water.
• Reduce further moisture loss by placing vegetables in plastic bags or storage boxes or wrapping them in a damp tea-towel or kitchen paper.
• Store in a cool, dark place such as the salad box of a refrigerator.

Week 4

> **Leave your courgettes for a few days and you could be faced with a multitude of overgrown marrows**

Midsummer review

This is a good time to take a look at your vegetable plot and see just how things are going. There should be plenty to harvest over the midsummer period, but are you soon going to end up with some gaps? And what can you do to fill them?

Certain crops will, with the right care, carry on cropping for the whole season from a single sowing or planting. Runner beans are one of the most efficient crops you can grow, and as long as you keep picking the pods they should carry on right through until the first frosts. As the plants become more and more prolific, our enthusiasm for harvesting can flag a little, but it really is worth picking every pod you can find. If you allow some of the pods to ripen their seeds, the plant will take this as a signal that its job is done and it will stop cropping.

You should be able to keep courgettes and summer squashes going until the end of the summer, too. Again, they need to be looked over frequently, as courgettes have a habit of turning into monster marrows in a very short time.

Other crops have a shorter harvest. Peas and French beans will crop well for a few weeks, but eventually the plants will run out of steam and need replacing. Crops such as lettuce, beetroot, carrots and summer cabbage have just a single harvest; once they are gone, they leave behind a gap which needs to be filled.

Take a look at your current crops and estimate the likely harvest time for each of them. Make a note of when space is likely to become free, and then decide how you can make most use of it. There is still time to make sowings of fast-maturing crops and plant out winter vegetables.

Crops that can be sown to fill gaps
Beetroot
Chinese greens
Calabrese
Carrot
Chicory
Corn salad
Endive
Florence fennel
French beans
Parsley
Lettuce
Onions for overwintering
Peas
Radish (including winter varieties)
Spinach, spinach beet and Swiss chard
Salad onion
Sprouting broccoli
Turnips

Crops that can be transplanted to fill gaps
Broccoli
Brussels sprouts
Autumn and winter cabbage
Calabrese
Cauliflower
Florence fennel
Kale
Leek
Lettuce

Right: Crops such as leeks can be transplanted to fill the gaps where earlier crops have been harvested.

Coping with a glut

Sooner or later in the next few weeks there will come a point when you have just too much produce to eat while it's still fresh. There is no need to waste anything, though – if you can see you won't be able to use your harvest before its quality starts to deteriorate, one of the best ways of preserving it is by freezing.

Freezing is not suitable for all crops. Tomatoes and courgettes lose their shape and collapse when they are thawed, and frozen lettuce doesn't bear thinking about! But even with difficult crops, you can often turn them into a cooked dish that will freeze very successfully. Tomatoes, aubergines, courgettes and peppers make a good ratatouille, and even lettuce can be frozen in the form of lettuce soup.

Preparation

Most vegetables are prepared as though for cooking before freezing; runner beans should be sliced, peas podded,

Left: A glut of courgettes or marrows can be turned into a delicious ratatouille for freezing.

carrots scrubbed, and so on. The majority of vegetables will benefit from being blanched – plunged into boiling water for two or three minutes, then rapidly cooled. This step is not essential but it does improve the quality of the frozen produce.

Pack the vegetables into meal-sized portions in plastic bags or freezer boxes, and label with the variety and date. Freeze as quickly as possible, turning on the boost switch if your freezer has one.

Vegetables suitable for freezing

It's not worth freezing vegetables such as mature carrots, beetroot and potatoes, which store quite well anyway, but you might want to freeze baby beet, new potatoes and whole young carrots. Beet should be boiled until tender and skinned; potatoes and carrots are best par-boiled for a few minutes. Their flavour won't be quite the same as fresh, but they will be a nice reminder of early summer later in the year. Other veg suitable for freezing are asparagus, broccoli, cabbage, cauliflower, herbs, onions, peas, peppers and spinach, and broad, French and runner beans.

DRIED TOMATOES

Though it's quite difficult to get them just right, sun-dried tomatoes can be made at home and if you have lots of tomatoes it's worth experimenting. We don't get enough sun for drying, so preheat the oven to 95°C/200°F/Gas mark 1. Slice the tomatoes thickly (or halve if small) and place on a baking sheet lined with baking parchment. Put this in the oven and leave the door slightly ajar. Check them every few hours until they are dry and leathery but not hard – this usually takes between four and eight hours.

Enjoying your garden

The vegetable garden is not just a place to work – it's also a place to interact with nature. To watch the drama of the seasons unfold, and to be directly affected by it through what we grow, builds a deep connection with the real world. Every so often we need to pause from our weeding, planting or digging, and take the time to really appreciate the natural world around us.

So an integral part of the vegetable garden should be a little area where we can relax and take our ease; to sit for a few quiet moments with a cup of tea and simply listen to the birdsong or watch the bees busy among the bean flowers.

Take a look at any allotment site, and it's very likely you will see that nearly every plot contains a ramshackle shed. This shed is not just a place for storing tools and fertilizers – it often also contains a folding chair, and perhaps a camping stove and a kettle for that all-important brew.

A sociable space

In our own gardens it's nice to make our leisure space a bit more pleasing to the eye. An attractive, comfortable seat is the first step: a wooden or metal seat that can stay out all year is a better idea

than one that needs to be put away in winter. Make a firm, clean area for it to stand on – paving slabs, bricks, decking or gravel will all do the job. Set the seat in a sheltered, warm position with a good view, so that you can appreciate the best points of your vegetable plot as you relax.

Some form of shelter makes it a great place to get out of a summer shower or the biting wind for a little while. The shelter could be anything from a sturdy garden parasol to an open-sided loggia or a splendid timber chalet – whatever you can afford or will suit your garden.

Finally, make sure there is seating for more than one person. When your vegetable garden is in full, beautiful production in the summer months, you may find your little haven attracts visitors who are keen to admire the view, and it can become a very sociable space. With a little luck, you'll even be able to persuade your visitors to lend a hand with the weeding while they are there!

Right: When you have worked hard to keep your vegetable garden productive and attractive, it's important to find the space and time simply to sit down and appreciate it.

AUGUST

" 'Keep it coming' could be the clarion call for the dog days of August. There is more harvesting than sowing now, and the fresh verdancy of May has given way to saturated green splashed here and there with vibrant colour as tomatoes and peppers begin to redden, squash and pumpkins start to ripen and borlotti and purple and yellow beans hang down, showing off their handsome pods.

Watering, feeding, tidying and clearing are the order of the day. There is juggling to be done – shall I take out the lettuce and rocket sown in June now or is there more to harvest before it is replaced with fresh salad? Are the beans growing around the sweetcorn in 'the three sisters' bed strangling their hosts? Should green manure be sown now or is there some immediately profitable crop that can be grown quickly, leaving its sowing till later?

Crops for immediate consumption must be gathered as they ripen, trying to keep abreast of fast-maturing beans, courgettes and tomatoes. This is a good time to exchange with friends and neighbours and swapping produce and observations enriches the gardening experience.

This is the month of the harvest moon and there are long balmy evenings to sit out and eat, enjoying the garden and its bounty. It is fruition time. There is so much to harvest, you can allow yourself the indulgence of paper-thin shaved fennel for salads, courgette flowers stuffed with fragrant rice, and herb-flecked artichoke hearts sitting in tepid olive oil; on holiday in your own garden.

Jobs for August

Sow for next spring Early in the month, sow next spring's cabbages, leaf beet and spring onions.

Pinch out herb flowers Keep removing the flowers on herbs so that the plants produce extra leaves.

Harvest garlic, onions and shallots When ready, the leaves will turn yellow and fall, and the produce can be gathered, dried and stored.

Tomatoes Tie tomatoes on to their supports. Nip out side shoots and tops of upright tomatoes; the bush types do not need sideshooting.

Remove runner beans Pinch out the tips of climbing beans as they reach the top of their support. This encourages them to concentrate on producing pods.

Stake winter brassicas Tall winter crops like Brussels sprouts and purple sprouting broccoli can be earthed up or staked to secure them against winter gales in exposed gardens.

Plant out seedlings Crops raised in early summer should be planted out now.

Plant new potatoes for autumn It is worth making a planting now, even though blight can be damaging in a wet, warm autumn.

Pests and diseases Attacks often decrease in hot, dry weather, but caterpillars can be very damaging to cabbage family crops if they are allowed to develop. Potato blight remains a risk in wet periods. Affected potato crops should have their foliage removed and disposed of; the potatoes should be lifted two weeks later. Don't ignore carrot fly – it's still a potential problem and an infestation can ruin the roots.

Sow green manures If you have spare time and space and the soil is sufficiently moist, sow fodder radish, fenugreek, and mustard, for example, to improve soil fertility and the workability of stiff ground.

Greenhouse tomatoes Keep pinching out sideshoots, and pinch out the tops of plants at the end of the month so they concentrate on ripening the fruits already set. If whitefly is a problem, sticky yellow cards will trap large numbers of the flying insects.

Vegetable showing This is the month when most local vegetable shows take place. If you want to have a go at showing your produce, make sure your entry complies with the show schedule. If you don't feel confident enough to take part, go along anyway and find out what it's all about – it might inspire you for next year!

Clear up thoroughly Clear spent crops promptly once the harvest has been gathered to eliminate pests and diseases, and expose weeds.

Week 1

Tomatoes

Hundreds of tomato varieties are available, from tiny cherry tomatoes to the giant beefsteaks; from yellow to red to purple; round, flattened or plum shaped. It can make for a lifetime of experimentation!

Tomato tips

• Tomatoes need heat to be successful. If you grow outdoor varieties, choose the right variety, start them off early and give them the warmest spot you've got.

• Plants in a greenhouse, conservatory or even a porch or cheap polythene tunnel will fruit earlier and for longer.

• If tomatoes are likely to occupy the same site for several years, as in a greenhouse bed, it is best to grow them in containers or growing bags to prevent pests and diseases building up in the soil.

• Dry conditions can cause blossom end rot, a troublesome disease whereby part of the fruit becomes blackened. Avoid this by watering regularly.

Recommended varieties

'Sungold': An exceptionally sweet, orange-red cherry tomato that does best if given some protection.

'Outdoor Girl AGM': Classic round red tomatoes of good flavour. Outdoor.

'Gardener's Delight AGM': Cherry tomatoes with an exceptionally sweet flavour on long trusses. Will grow either under glass or outside in a warm spot.

'Summer Sweet AGM': Heavy, early crops of attractive small red, juicy plum tomatoes. Outdoors or under glass.

Week **2**

❝The tomato was once regarded as an aphrodisiac, and known as the love apple or pomme d'amour❞

Stuffed peppers

Peppers like the same sort of conditions as tomatoes, and while they love the warmth of a greenhouse, they also grow well in pots and growing bags on a sunny patio. If green peppers are left on the plant, they will ripen to red (or yellow or orange, depending on variety), but leaving fruit to mature on the plant does reduce the yield.

Ingredients

Serves 4

4 large green peppers
1 tablespoon olive oil
1 onion, finely chopped
50g (2oz) rindless streaky bacon, finely chopped
175g (6oz) lean minced beef
4 tablespoons breadcrumbs
1 egg, beaten
1 tablespoon chopped fresh parsley
salt and pepper

SAUCE
2 tablespoons olive oil
340g (¾lb) skinned and chopped fresh tomatoes or one 250g (8oz) can tomatoes
1 tablespoon tomato purée
1 garlic clove, crushed
1 teaspoon brown sugar
1 tablespoon wine vinegar

Method

Preheat the oven to 160°C/325°F/ Gas mark 3.

Cut the tops off the peppers and reserve. Scoop out the seeds with a spoon. Heat the oil in a saucepan and sauté the onion for 5 minutes. Stir in the bacon and beef and cook, turning, for 5 more minutes. Stir in the breadcrumbs. Remove the pan from the heat, stir in the egg and parsley and season with salt and pepper to taste. Stuff the peppers with this mixture, stand them upright in a deep ovenproof dish and replace the tops.

To prepare the sauce, gently heat the oil in a small pan, add the fresh or canned tomatoes and tomato purée and mix well. Add all of the remaining ingredients, season to taste and bring to the boil. Reduce the heat, cover and cook gently, stirring occasionally, for 10 minutes.

Pour the sauce over the peppers, cover and cook in the oven for about 40 minutes. Serve hot.

Week 3

Fruit for the vegetable plot

Left: A delicious strawberry crop can be grown in containers.

mulch, which keeps weeds at bay, conserves soil moisture and helps keep fruit clean. Keep the soil moist at all times and liquid feed with a high potash fertilizer once the fruits start to form. Protect fruit from both birds and slugs. Strawberries are ideal for growing in containers and even growing bags.

Blueberries

These need acid soil, and are often best grown in containers filled with ericaceous (lime-free) compost. Use as large a container as you have room for, and keep the compost moist at all times, preferably using rainwater. You will need to protect the fruit from birds. Prune out some of the older stems each winter.

Currants and gooseberries

Currants and gooseberries are easy to grow, but watch out for mildew, which can spoil the gooseberry crop. Blackcurrants bear a heavy crop of tasty berries; redcurrants have a lovely sharp flavour and look like sparkling jewels. If more than one bush is required, allow about 1.5m (5ft) between plants.

Tree fruits such as apples and pears usually need a reasonably sized garden, but many types of soft fruit are easy to fit into the vegetable plot. A sunny sheltered position is best; but as birds are also fond of soft fruit, an area that can be enclosed in netting or a fruit cage is useful.

Like vegetables, fruit prefers a fertile, moisture-retentive but free-draining soil. Several types can be grown in pots; a rich compost like John Innes potting compost is usually best for containers.

Strawberries

A strawberry bed should ideally be replaced every three or four years for the best crops. August is the best month for planting. A popular method is to plant through a plastic sheet

Cane fruits

These include raspberries, blackberries and the hybrid berries such as tayberry and loganberry. They need some form of permanent supports, such as posts and wires, but will continue cropping for many years with the right treatment.

Week 4

Perennial crops

Perennial vegetables, like herbaceous perennials, die down at the end of the year and re-sprout the following spring. They are are ideal for beginners since they don't need specialist care and provide excellent value, cropping for many years.

Artichokes

Globe artichokes need a sunny, sheltered site with well-drained, moisture-retentive soil to which plenty of organic matter has been added. Buy small pot-grown plants and space them 1m (3ft) apart, ideally during spring or autumn. In their first year, weed and water plants well and remove any flower heads produced.

Globe artichokes crop best in their second and third years. If one large flower head is required, remove the side shoots on each flower stem. Cut the artichokes with secateurs before the scales start to open, or they will be tough.

Cut off rooted offsets (young plants which attach to the parent) with a sharp knife in early spring and replant them. Use these to replace plants after their third year.

Asparagus

The 'all-male' F1 hybrid varieties are the most productive. Choose a sunny, sheltered site with well-drained soil, and dig in plenty of organic matter before planting.

Crowns are available for planting in early spring and sometimes in autumn. Apply a balanced organic fertilizer and a 5cm (2in) thick mulch of organic matter in early spring before the spears emerge.

Do not cut any emerging spears the first year. One-year-old crowns of F1 hybrids can be harvested for six weeks one year after planting (or two if they are open pollinated), and for eight weeks in subsequent years. After this, allow the fern to develop and cut it down to the base when it has turned completely yellow in autumn.

Rhubarb

Provide a sunny position and well-drained but moisture-retentive, weed-free, fertile soil that has had plenty of organic matter added. Rhubarb can be bought as dormant crowns for planting in late autumn, or pot-grown plants, which can be planted any time but ideally in spring or autumn. Don't harvest any stems until the second year.

Stems can be harvested until midsummer, after which they become rather tough and green. Stopping then also allows the plant to produce sufficient foliage to build up food reserves for next year. Remove no more than half the stalks at any one time, harvesting as soon as the leaves open fully.

Top left: Covering rhubarb stems with a forcing pot will make them even more tender.

Top right: Succulent asparagus spears will start to push their way through the soil in spring.

Bottom: Globe artichokes make statuesque plants that are decorative as well as productive.

Ornamental veg

If you have a small garden, you will want every bit of it to look attractive – and that includes the vegetable plot. Fortunately, there are plenty of vegetables that have good looks as well as a good flavour.

A well-planned, formal decorative vegetable garden can look stunning, but needs a lot of care. Weeds and pests have to be rigidly controlled and harvesting any of your carefully grown specimens may ruin the overall display. It's a lot easier to opt for a slightly less formal effect. Growing decorative vegetables in among the flowers can be very attractive; try a wigwam of scarlet-flowered runner beans, an edging of curly leaved parsley or a globe artichoke in the flower border.

Particularly attractive vegetables include leeks, with their bold blue symmetrically arranged fountain of

Left: Mixing rows of vegetables and flowers of contrasting colours can add an extra decorative touch to companion planting.

leaves; asparagus pea, which has pretty, ferny leaves and reddish-brown flowers followed by unusual winged pods; Swiss chard, with deeply quilted leaves and colourful leaf stems; lettuce in many varieties; courgettes, especially those with yellow fruits; bush tomatoes; purple kohl rabi and many more.

Show time

If you are planning to enter your produce at the local show, this is the time to make sure you are on the right track.

Select your potential prizewinners well before the show date and ensure they are not likely to get damaged before the big day. Support items like marrows and pumpkins on a piece of wood or tile to raise them off the ground. Break a leaf over the top of cauliflowers to shade them from the sun and keep the heads pearly white.

When picking produce on show day, be careful to handle it as little as possible; peas, for example, should be handled only by the stem to avoid spoiling the 'bloom' on the pods.

CAROL'S BEST BUYS

Some of my favourite ornamental vegetable varieties include French bean 'Valdo'; courgette 'One Ball'; lettuce 'Lollo Rossa'; kale 'Nero di Toscana'; summer squash 'Polo'; Swiss chard 'Bright Lights' and tomato 'Tumbling Tom'.

Summer care for containers

Containers of all types have only a limited amount of compost in them, and this means that vegetables can soon run short of both water and nutrients. Now that most container veg are in full crop, it's important to keep them going as long as possible.

Watering and feeding

Containers need watering frequently throughout the growing season, and there must be no let-up now. Once plants are fully grown, their leaves often completely cover the container, making it difficult for rainfall to penetrate through to the compost, so you can never rely on rain alone. If compost is ever allowed to dry out, it can be difficult to re-wet, and can seriously affect the crop. Blossom-end rot on tomatoes is a sure sign that the plants have gone short of water at a crucial stage in their fruit formation.

To check if a plant needs a drink, scrape away a little of the surface compost and see how moist it is underneath. When necessary, water thoroughly until the water starts to come through the drainage holes.

Because container-grown plants need frequent watering, nutrients tend to be quickly washed out of the compost. If you added a slow-release fertilizer to the compost at planting time, this will help make sure your plants receive a steady supply of nutrients. Otherwise, a general-purpose liquid feed can be added to the water throughout the growing season. Fruiting crops, such as tomatoes, peppers and courgettes, need a high-potash liquid feed such as tomato fertilizer, which helps the production and development of flowers and fruits. This should have been started as soon as the crop started to set, and should continue now until the end of the season.

General care of container crops

Make sure that any diseased leaves or other parts of plants are removed promptly, particularly when the weather is warm and humid, as these conditions are ideal for the spread of fungal diseases. Check that plant supports are still doing their job, and renew them if necessary. Keep an eye out for slugs and snails, which can hide among groups of containers and do a great deal of damage, particularly in wet spells of weather. Treat insect pests such as aphids where necessary, too.

Top left: Tomatoes in containers need regular watering and feeding throughout the season.

Top right: Fruiting crops like courgettes will benefit from a high-potash liquid feed.

Bottom: Well-cared for container-grown plants like this chilli pepper can produce heavy crops.

SEPTEMBER

" The weather is changing. Dew sparkles on ripening pumpkins and for the first time in months there is a slight sense of decay, of the beginning of the end. Underlying the slowdown though, is a rounding off, a sense of completing the circle. The air is scented with the aroma of ripening fruit and full-blown flowers.

This is a time to savour and reflect on what the year has given us. Inevitability is the key word. It's too late now to adjust or compensate, but a season to indulge, appreciate, enjoy – and harvest. As pumpkins, squashes and marrows swell and their skin thickens and hardens, they are severed from their shrivelling vines and left to toughen up. On hot sunny days – and don't there seem to be more and more of them in September? – they can be turned over to bake. The pods of haricot and borlotti beans are beginning to brown and curl, and podding them and extracting the hard, perfect beans is one of the most satisfying of September's jobs – not work at all, more a treasure hunt.

Storing crops, whether it be boxes of carrots or beetroot, clamps of potatoes or big glass jars full of dried beans or peas is not only hugely satisfying – verging on the self-righteous – but it is also a link with our past. Our not-so-distant ancestors, before the advent of refrigeration and canning, depended for their winter food on stored vegetables. There is always a feeling of satisfaction in seeing the fruits of your labours stock-piled for the coming winter while outside the vegetable garden still basks in the last days of an Indian summer. "

Jobs for September

Harvest potatoes Maincrop potatoes will be ready this month; if you leave them in the ground too long, slugs will damage the tubers so that they won't store. Choose a sunny, dry day for the harvest, lift the potatoes with a fork and leave them on the soil surface for a few hours to dry before putting them in hessian or paper sacks and storing in a dark cool place. Sort out any damaged potatoes and use these straight away – don't try to store them, as they will rot.

Plant autumn onion sets Plant sets late this month for the earliest crop next year. Only a few varieties are available for autumn planting; 'Senshyu' is a well-established Japanese variety and 'Radar' is also very popular. 'Swift' is perhaps the earliest, maturing from late May. Plant the sets in a sheltered place in free-draining soil.

Compost garden debris Home-made compost is a brilliant soil improver, adding valuable organic matter. Put all your garden debris onto a compost heap except for diseased plants and pernicious weeds like bindweed.

Harvest sweetcorn Test to see if cobs are ripe by peeling back the sheath and piercing a kernel with your thumb; if it exudes a milky liquid, it's ready to eat. Don't cut the cobs until the saucepan of water is on the boil – cook and eat them within minutes for the sweetest flavour.

Blossom end rot A shrunken, black, inedible area forms at the base of tomatoes, and occasionally peppers, when plants have run short of water while the fruit was setting and swelling. There is nothing that can be done once the symptoms are seen, but in future make sure you keep plants evenly moist at all times.

Lift maincrop carrots In light soils, carrots keep quite well in the ground, but in heavier, slug-infested soils, they are best lifted and stored in boxes of sand or loam.

Sow winter lettuce Varieties such as 'Winter Density', 'Arctic King' and 'Valdor' will overwinter outside in sheltered areas to give a spring harvest.

Continue regular harvesting Keep picking beans, courgettes, cucumbers and so on while they are still young and tender. They soon become stringy and not so good to eat at this time of year. Lettuce should also be harvested promptly, or it will start to go to seed and become bitter.

Week 1

Sweetcorn

Harvested at its peak, sweetcorn has a superlative flavour. No matter how hard they try, supermarkets and greengrocers can't compete with a cob that has been harvested, cooked and eaten within the hour.

Sweetcorn tips

• For an early crop in cold areas, sow seed indoors in a large module or small pot and plant out when all danger of frost has gone. In warm areas, sow seeds where they are to grow in late spring and early summer. Choose a sheltered, sunny site with well-drained soil.

• Grow sweetcorn in blocks to ensure good pollination. Make blocks at least four plants deep and wide, with each plant 35–45cm (14–18in) apart.

• Supersweet varieties have been bred to have especially sweet, tender kernels. If you cultivate these, you mustn't also grow the older cultivars because cross-pollination causes the kernels to turn starchy.

• Once the tassels on the ends of the cobs turn brown, peel back the husk to check the corn. When ready to be picked, it will be pale yellow, and a milky liquid will appear when a kernel is pricked.

Recommended varieties

'Lark' AGM: Fairly early-maturing, extra-tender sweet variety with large cobs of uniformly yellow, soft-textured kernels.

'Swift' AGM: Early, extra-tender variety with a deliciously sweet flavour. Said to grow well in cool climates.

Week 2

"Sweetcorn plants love each other's company, so plant them in a block rather than rows"

Fresh vegetable pizza

September is the month when you will have an embarrassment of riches from the vegetable garden. You can use all kinds of veg in this pizza and it's a great way of getting children to eat their five-a-day without fuss. If you are in a hurry, you can buy ready-made pizza bases in most supermarkets.

Ingredients

Serves 4

PIZZA BASE

250g (8oz) self-raising flour
1 teaspoon salt
150 ml (¼ pint) warm water

TOPPING

5 tablespoons olive oil
2 garlic cloves, crushed
1 red onion, finely sliced
2 courgettes, thinly sliced lengthways
1 red pepper, cored, deseeded and cut into strips
1 yellow pepper, cored, deseeded and cut into strips
4 tomatoes, skinned, cored and cut into wedges
2 large handfuls spinach leaves, washed and wilted in a saucepan
4 sprigs thyme, separated into leaves
1 handful basil leaves, roughly torn
salt and pepper

Method

Preheat the oven to 230°C/450°F/ gas mark 8. To make the pizza base, place the flour and salt in a large bowl. Slowly add the water and mix to form a soft dough. When it has bound together, use your hands to form it into a ball. Turn the dough out on a lightly floured surface and knead until smooth and soft.

Divide the dough into four pieces and, with your hands and a rolling pin, flatten each as thinly as possible. The pizza rounds do not have to be exact circles. Make the pizzas a little bit smaller than your serving plates.

Put the pizza bases onto warmed baking sheets, brush with a little of the olive oil, then arrange the vegetables on the bases, sprinkling them with the thyme leaves and roughly torn basil.

Season the pizzas generously with salt and pepper, drizzle with the remaining olive oil, and bake at the top of the oven for 10 minutes. The vegetables should be slightly charred around the edges, as this adds to the flavour.

Week 3

Crops for forcing and blanching

Some vegetables can be blanched by excluding light as they are growing. This makes the vegetables more tender and prevents bitterness from developing. Forcing is when plants are helped to produce an earlier crop by protecting them from the weather and providing extra warmth. Forcing and blanching can go hand in hand.

Blanching can be carried out outside, where the crops are growing. Exclude light either by gathering the leaves together and tying them with string to produce a blanched heart (for example, like sugarloaf chicory), or by earthing plants up, as with celery and leeks, or by placing a bucket or pot over them, as with rhubarb.

Placing a forcing pot or bucket over a plant also tends to speed its growth by providing a little extra weather protection, especially if you first add an insulating covering of straw or dry leaves. But to advance the crop even more, it can be brought into a warmer place such as a frost-free greenhouse.

To force rhubarb, dig a crown up in the next few weeks, once it has become dormant, and leave it on the soil surface until it has been thoroughly frosted. Pot it up in moist potting compost and take it into a frost-free greenhouse or shed. Cover with a lightproof bucket or black polythene on supports, and tender pink stalks will be ready for pulling in about six or seven weeks.

Whitloof chicory can be treated in a similar way, except the roots don't need

Above: Terracotta forcing pots are attractive as well as functional, but unfortunately they are also expensive and difficult to obtain.

to be frosted – just trim off the leaves before potting up the roots. Fat chicons will be ready for cutting when they are about 18cm (7in) tall. It's very important to exclude all light from chicons or they will be unpleasantly bitter.

A more unusual crop for forcing is seakale, a member of the cabbage family that produces slender, creamy stems when blanched; cook them lightly and serve with butter, like asparagus.

Forcing pots

Although old dustbins or buckets do the job of excluding light well enough, a purpose-made rhubarb forcing pot does it with much more style. These tall, cylindrical pots are made of terracotta and usually have a removable lid.

Forcing pots were popular in Victorian times and old ones are occasionally available at antique auctions. Some small independent potteries also make them.

Week 4

> **The secret underground bounty of root vegetables will sustain you through the winter months**

Harvesting mature vegetables

Vegetables that are to be stored for use during the winter usually need to be fully mature before they are harvested, or they won't store well. There are a number of crops that will be maturing now and over the next few weeks, so you will be kept busy gathering and storing them.

Onions

Harvesting onions is one of my favourite jobs. There is a wonderful moment when you realize that all those luscious green stems have toppled over, as if they've given their all. Use a fork to loosen the bulbs from the soil, and then spread the bulbs out in the sun to dry, ideally on wire mesh above the ground so that air can circulate around them. Once the bulbs are dry, gently knock off any loose soil and leaves, then store them in a net bag in a cool, dry shed or garage. The remnants of stems and leaves also make a convenient tool for bunching or plaiting them together, and hanging them ready for use.

Potatoes

Early, 'new' potatoes have skins that can be rubbed off with your thumb, but maincrop potatoes for storing must have skins that are 'set' and firm to the touch. About two weeks before you intend to harvest the crop, cut off the top growth (called the haulm); this encourages the skins to firm up. Dig the crop on a dry, sunny day, and leave the potatoes on the soil surface for a few hours to dry. Remove any damaged

tubers and use these up straight away; the rest of the crop can be stored in hessian or paper sacks in a cool, dry, dark place. Never use plastic sacks, as these trap moisture and cause the potatoes to rot.

Pumpkins, squashes and beans

Pumpkins, winter squashes and mature marrows need to develop a tough, hard skin to ensure they keep well. Leave them on the plant for as long as possible, at the same time protecting them from any danger of frost. Cut the ripe fruits off the plant with a good length of stalk. 'Cure' the fruits in a sunny, warm, dry place such as a greenhouse or cold frame for 10 days, before storing in a cool, dry place.

Finally, beans grown for their dried seeds rather than their pods, such as borlotti beans, need harvesting this month. The pods become dry and brittle and start to split open when the beans are ripe. Harvest them on a sunny day, shell them and leave the beans in an airy place to dry thoroughly before storing them in paper bags or airtight containers.

Top: Bunch onions together by their dried leaves if you want to hang them up in store.

Bottom left: Several root crops such as celeriac can safely be left in the ground all winter.

Bottom right: Winter squashes that have been properly cured will store well in a cool, dry place.

Making pickles and chutneys

There is something very satisfying about converting your garden produce into rows of gleaming jars filled with home-made pickles and preserves. It's a great way of coping with a glut, and if you use pretty jars with decorative tops they make lovely Christmas presents for friends.

Preserves make use of sugar, vinegar and salt to prevent food spoiling. Pickles are vegetables preserved in vinegar; the vegetables usually keep their shape and have a pleasant crunch. Chutneys contain both vinegar and sugar and some form of fruit along with the vegetables. The ingredients are chopped and cooked until they combine to form a jam-like substance with a mellow flavour.

Pickles

Wash the vegetables and cut them into suitable-size pieces. Make a brine from 100g salt to 1 litre (4oz to 2 pints) water and soak the vegetables for 24 hours. Drain well and pack into clean jars; cover with spiced vinegar and an airtight lid. Spiced vinegar can be bought ready made, or you can make your own by adding pickling spices to hot vinegar, allowing it to cool, and steeping for 12 hours before straining and bottling.

Suitable vegetables for pickling include cauliflower florets, beetroot, onions, courgettes, cucumber and red cabbage. A mixed vegetable piccalilli is great for using up whatever you have too much of.

Chutneys

There are lots of different recipes for chutneys in any good cookbook. The fruit and vegetables used should be chopped finely and cooked gently in a large pan until they are soft, then vinegar, sugar and spices are added and the mixture cooked over a low heat until it has reached the right consistency. The hot chutney is put in clean, pre-warmed jars and covered with waxed paper circles and a close-fitting lid.

Chutneys can use a mix of almost any vegetables you have to hand. Onions and garlic are nearly always included; tomatoes (especially green ones), peppers, aubergines, celery, cucumbers, marrows, rhubarb, beans, leeks and pumpkins are just a few of the possibilities. Apples are always a favourite for the fruit content, but plums are also excellent.

Bottling

Bottling uses special jars that form a vacuum seal to keep the contents fresh. The only vegetable it is safe to bottle at home is the tomato, which contains sufficient acid to kill bacteria – other vegetables may cause food poisoning if bottled. Special instructions for bottling can be found in cookbooks, and must be followed carefully.

Left: Bottling jars enable a vacuum seal to be formed in order to keep the contents fresh.

Raised beds

A raised bed in the garden or on a patio can increase the range and quantity of vegetables grown. Think of a raised bed as a large, specially constructed container with no base, made of wood or brick. If you can get to the RHS garden at Harlow Carr, be inspired by taking a look at their raised beds built on a 3 x 3m (10 x 10ft) plot to demonstrate what is possible in a small area.

Advantages of a raised bed

• The growing area is concentrated in a permanent bed with easy access from a permanent path.
• The soil warms up quite quickly and can be worked on for more days of the year than open-ground beds.
• It's possible to plant closer and still get good yields because plants are growing in soil with high fertility, and there is extra light from the sides.
• You can fill the raised bed with the most appropriate soil for your crop.
• One raised bed is a much less daunting prospect than a large vegetable plot that needs planning, planting and maintaining.
• Beds can be made to almost any shape. Different materials can be used to match the style and size of the garden.

Disadvantages of a raised bed

• The time, expense and effort needed to build them can be a burden and constructing them is not an easy task.
• Once in place, they cannot be moved easily.
• They dry out more quickly than open-ground beds, requiring watering and mulching in dry weather.
• Significantly, there are plenty of hiding places in the sides for potential pests, like slugs and snails.

Choosing the size and shape

Ideally, beds should be no wider than 1.2m (4ft) so that they can be comfortably worked from both sides. Square or rectangular beds make the best use of a small space and are easier to construct. You can buy ready-made raised beds (wooden or recycled plastic), which have the great advantage of being easy and quick to construct, but doing it yourself is cheaper and gives your design flexibility.

The sides are most commonly made of wood, but can be in other materials such as stone blocks. Fill the bed with good quality topsoil mixed with organic matter. The soil must be free-draining and open textured. You can buy in topsoil if you do not have your own soil or it is not suitable.

Top left: Raised beds can be an attractive and practical feature in the vegetable garden.

Top right: Make the beds about 1.2m (4ft) wide so that you can reach the middle from either side.

Bottom: If you are making your raised bed from bricks, remember to leave weep holes in the walls for drainage.

OCTOBER

"What a change October brings. If it is kind, there are bright warm days that feel as though late summer could last forever, then suddenly they are interrupted by a rude cold snap that warns us not to be too complacent. Not only does the the weather change from calm to tempest, but temperatures can plummet without warning, plunging us into panic. The first frost spells curtains for tender crops. Tomatoes should be hastily picked, the green ones put into drawers to ripen, and ripe fruit consumed now or combined with the last of the courgettes, peppers and aubergines to make huge pots of ratatouille to last into the dark days of winter.

Though growth has slowed down, annual weeds will seize any opportunity to spread their seed. They should be pulled out and burned, or if they are younger, cut down with a sharp hoe and left to shrivel on a warm day.

Turn any remaining onions over for the last few times, sometimes on the ground, but more often on wattle panels or wooden boxes, to enjoy the last of the glorious sunshine. Later plait them or simply tie in bunches.

It's not all doom and gloom though, the soil is still warm and winter salad crops can be planted out from modules and even sown direct. It's worth experimenting with green manure and using this opportunity to think about putting back the goodness that has given us the year's bounty."

Jobs for October

Watch out for frosts Depending on where you garden, the first frosts will probably arrive some time this month. Make sure that you are prepared!

Harvest outdoor tomatoes Pick the entire trusses of any fruit that are left and move them indoors or into the greenhouse to ripen. Pull up the plants and compost them, unless they show signs of blight, in which case they should be burnt.

Protect brassicas As the weather becomes colder, pigeons are likely to attack winter brassicas like cabbage and Brussels sprouts. Protect plants with fleece or netting. If pigeons are a serious problem in your area, think about growing winter brassicas in a fruit cage.

Harvest pumpkins and winter squashes These need to be harvested before a hard frost. Make sure the skins are firm, then cut the fruits and leave them in a bright warm place (such as a greenhouse or sunroom) for 10 days to 'cure' before they are stored in a dry, cool, but frost-free place.

Plant garlic This does best in a free-draining soil and in a sunny site.

Warm the soil If you intend to sow broad beans outside for overwintering, place cloches over the sowing area in order to keep off rain and warm the soil.

Parsnips Although these are big enough to eat now, it's best to leave them until late autumn or winter – they keep perfectly well in the ground, and you will be glad of them when there are few other vegetables about. Parsnips are always said to taste sweeter after a few hard frosts.

Protect winter lettuce Use cloches to protect winter lettuces sown last month if the weather turns cold.

Pick remaining runner beans The long runner bean season is drawing to an end. Pods that have been missed will have developed bumps where the seeds are forming. The pods are tough and stringy and not worth eating, but the developing beans inside them are quite tasty.

Compost runner bean topgrowth The above-ground haulms (stems) are excellent material for the compost heap, but the roots can be left in the ground to be dug in later – they add nitrogen to the soil.

Start forcing Plump white chicons are very good for winter salads, so start forcing witloof chicory, but you must exclude all light while they are developing, or they will be very bitter.

Week 1

> The flavour of home-grown potatoes is so concentrated, so earthy, it's completely different from the bland supermarket varieties

Pumpkins

Pumpkins are just what you want in your larder as the weather turns cold: perfectly ripened fruits, all wonderfully autumnal.

Pumpkin tips
• Plants are frost-tender, so you must sow seed indoors or in a frost-free greenhouse about one month before the last expected frost. Don't plant out until all risk of frost has passed.
• Look for early ripening cultivars – pumpkins need a long, hot growing season to ripen fully.
• To grow the largest possible pumpkin, leave one fruit on each plant and give it extra water and feed. As it swells, place it on pieces of wood or bricks to keep it off the wet soil and avoid pest attacks.

• Provide the sunniest, most sheltered spot and grow in moist, fertile soil that has been improved before planting with general-purpose fertilizer.
• Pumpkins store well over winter. Leave them on the plant for as long as possible to develop a tough skin, but protect them from frost. Store in a dry, cool, frost-free place.

Recommended varieties
'Becky': A classic orange, medium-sized Hallowe'en pumpkin, perfect for carving. Very prolific and high yielding.
'Hundredweight': Similar to Becky but much larger. Trailing habit.
'Rouge Vif d'Etamps': A really stunning pumpkin with red, ribbed skin and moist orange flesh. Vigorous, trailing growth.

Week 2

Green tomato chutney

At the end of the season you will doubtless be left with some unripened fruit – but don't throw your green tomatoes away. This chutney is delicious, and it will mature just in time to make Christmas gifts for friends and family.

Ingredients

1kg (2lb) green tomatoes, finely chopped
500g (1lb) onions, finely chopped
500g (1lb) cooking apples, peeled, cored and chopped
2 fresh green chillies, halved, deseeded and finely chopped
2 garlic cloves, crushed
1 teaspoon ground ginger
generous pinch of ground cloves
generous pinch of ground turmeric
50g (2oz) raisins
250g (8oz) soft dark brown sugar
300ml (½ pint) white wine vinegar

Method

Put the tomatoes, onions, apples and chillies into a large pan and mix together. Add the garlic, ginger, cloves and turmeric, then stir in the raisins, sugar and vinegar.

Bring to the boil, reduce the heat and cover the pan. Simmer, stirring frequently, for 1¼–1½ hours or until the chutney has thickened.

Transfer the chutney to warm dry jars and cover the surface of each with a disc of waxed paper, waxed side down, then top with an airtight lid. Label and leave to mature in a cool, dark place for at least 3 weeks before using, or store, unopened, for 6–12 months.

Week 3

> **What a difference there is between the vegetables we buy and those we grow!**

Pumpkin carving for Hallowe'en

Hallowe'en is a shortened form of 'All Hallows Eve', meaning the night before All Saints' Day on 1 November. But the real roots of this festival go right back to the ancient Celtic festival of *Samhain*, which was a celebration of the harvest and the end of the summer. Over the years, the Christian and pagan festivals have combined to give us Hallowe'en.

Above: Be imaginative when carving your pumpkin; there are lots of pictures on the internet to give you inspiration for your designs.

Because the dead were thought to walk the earth at this time, people used to light lanterns to guard against evil spirits, often carving a turnip as a holder for the light. European settlers took the lantern tradition to America, where they found the native pumpkins made a much better lantern than the turnip – and now pumpkin lanterns have become synonymous with the Hallowe'en festival on both sides of the Atlantic.

If you have grown your own pumpkins, it's always fun to carve a spooky face and set a flickering tea light inside – children love them! The best pumpkins for carving are medium-sized ones; the monsters are too difficult to carry, and their skins are often too tough to carve. Choose a pumpkin that has a flat base so that it will stand securely.

How to carve your pumpkin

Always use a really sharp blade for carving – most cut fingers result from having to put too much pressure on a blunt knife. First, cut a circle round the stem with a long-bladed knife so that you can detach a lid. Then scrape out the seeds and fibrous interior, making sure there is a flat area at the base to sit your light on. Draw your design on the pumpkin first, before you start cutting. Use a sharp but short-bladed knife that is easy to control. Don't just cut a simple oval shape for the mouth – leave one or two snaggle teeth. And don't make the mouth too low, or you will be able to see the candle at the base.

Once you have finished cutting your design, set your tea light or votive candle in a glass in the base. The easiest way to light it is with a taper, through the mouth. Set the lid back on top and enjoy the effect – but do keep an eye on it and make sure it stays safe while lit.

Week 4

Clearing the greenhouse

Greenhouse crops are now coming to an end, and it's time to start thinking about clearing up the greenhouse before the winter. It's important to do this, otherwise you will provide perfect conditions for all sorts of pests and diseases to overwinter, ready to start attacking your crops next spring.

Although you may have a few green tomatoes still hanging on your plants, it's not worth leaving them any longer. Pick off all the fruits and use them to make green tomato chutney, or take the larger ones into the house to ripen.

Remove all the growth of spent crops and put it on the compost heap (unless it is diseased). If plants have been growing in bags or containers, tip the contents of these on the compost heap, too. Dig over the soil in the greenhouse border and remove all weeds.

Pull out any pots and other equipment that is lurking under the staging, plus all the odds and ends that seem to accumulate in a greenhouse – packs of fertilizer, empty seed packets, old labels, string and so on. Throw away anything that is no longer useful, has got damp or damaged, or has lost its label. (If you are throwing out garden chemicals, contact your local council to arrange for their safe disposal.)

Sweep the greenhouse out, and with a stiff brush, brush down the staging and the greenhouse structure thoroughly. Remove any shading and clean the glass inside and out – you will want maximum light transmission in the winter.

On a sunny day, wash all the pots and seed trays and let them drain before stacking them back in your newly cleaned greenhouse.

If you are going to use your greenhouse for overwintering tender plants, it is worth lining the sides with bubble polythene for insulation – this will help to keep down the cost of heating. Always use a thermostatically controlled heater to avoid wasting fuel.

Right: If you do not clean your greenhouse thoroughly in autumn, it can provide the perfect overwintering place for a host of pests.

BIOLOGICAL CONTROL IN THE GREENHOUSE

It's possible to use pests' natural enemies to keep them under control in the greenhouse. These biological controls are bought from specialist suppliers in spring and can be effective if introduced early enough. Plants under glass are particularly susceptible to whitefly and red spider mite. *Encarsia formosa*, a tiny parasitic wasp, can be used against whitefly, while red spider mite can be controlled by *Phytoseiulus persimilis*, a predatory mite.

Preparing crops to overwinter

The cold winter weather will soon be upon us, and this is a good time to check on the crops that are still standing. Many hardy crops are quite happy to spend the winter in the ground; in fact, in many cases that is by far the best place for them. They will keep in good condition right through until the spring.

Crops that can normally be left in situ

Sprouting broccoli
Brussels sprouts
Winter and spring cabbages
Maincrop carrots
Winter cauliflowers
Celeriac
Jerusalem artichokes
Kale
Leeks
Parsnips
Salsify and scorzonera
Swede

However, there are exceptions. If you live in a really cold area, some crops might be damaged by penetrating frosts, though in all but the coldest regions, an insulating covering of straw held in place with fleece along the rows of root crops should do the trick. If your soil is very wet and heavy, you may well find root crops left in the ground will rot, or be ruined by slugs. In this case, it is a good idea to lift roots before the worst of the weather and store them more safely.

The best way to store lifted root crops is to twist off any topgrowth remaining and pack the roots in well-spaced layers in boxes of just-moist sand or peat substitute. Keep the boxes in a cool, frost-free shed.

It is always a good idea to have a few crops to hand ready for the really cold weather. When the ground is frozen solid, it becomes impossible to harvest crops like parsnips and leeks, which is most frustrating! Before the cold weather starts, lift a few days' supply and either store in a box, as above, or heel them into an area of light, free-draining soil where they will be easily accessible.

Autumn-sown broad beans and peas

In mild areas, an autumn sowing of broad beans and peas is worth trying for an extra-early summer crop next year. Only a few varieties are suitable; try pea 'Feltham First' or 'Kelvedon Wonder', and broad bean 'Aquadulce'. Sow from now through to mid-November, and protect the seedlings with cloches. Losses from these late sowings can be high, but in a good year you might be picking your first peas and beans in late May or early June.

Top: A commercial-sized polythene tunnel can be used to keep tender crops growing well into the autumn.

Bottom left: Low polythene tunnels or cloches are useful for protecting rows of autumn-sown peas and beans.

Bottom right: Winter cabbages are happy standing out in the vegetable garden through even the coldest weather.

NOVEMBER

“ Time to get out the scarves and the thermals, though there is plenty of exercise this month to keep us warm. November is all about thinking ahead, and preparing the ground – literally – for next year. In raised beds there is no need to dig – in fact, digging destroys the complex network of organisms that lead to soil fertility – but when gardening traditionally in the open ground, especially when it is heavy, turning over the soil and leaving it roughly dug allows frost to break it down and improve its texture. By next spring it should be much easier to break down and create the 'fine tilth' upon which we are all exhorted to sow our seeds. In raised beds and deep beds, muck can be laid direct onto the surface of the soil on the plots intended for legumes in the following season. If you have no access to muck, then any hearty organic matter will do, from spent mushroom compost to leaf mould.

In our garden we are surrounded by deciduous trees, and November is the great leaf-clearing month. We make big wire cages and pile up the leaves – this is the most effective way to create the rich, crumbly substance that adds humus to the soil so effectively. If you are not lucky enough to have access to masses of leaves, local councils can often provide road sweepings. The best leaves are oak and beech, although most deciduous leaves will eventually yield useable leaf mould.

Ground must be cleared now of summer crops and debris can be used instantly in the bottom of a trench for next year's runner beans. The cycle continues. ”

Jobs for November

Sow broad beans It is only worth making an autumn sowing of broad beans in reasonably mild areas – in cold, exposed gardens, wait until spring. Sow where cloches have been sheltering the soil, and use a hardy variety like 'Aquadulce' or 'The Sutton'.

Start winter digging As areas of the vegetable plot become vacant, dig them over and leave the soil in rough clods to be broken down by winter frosts.

Cover compost heaps Cover filled compost heaps with a layer of thick cardboard or old carpet to keep in the heat and keep out most of the rain. It pays to have two compost heaps; as soon as one is full, leave it to rot down while you start building the other one. Don't forget you can add kitchen waste to the heap, but avoid cooked food and meat, which can attract rats.

Revive rhubarb Old rhubarb crowns will benefit from being lifted and divided into sections with a sharp spade. Make sure each piece has some growth buds. Replant in soil that has been enriched with well-rotted compost or other organic matter.

Remove plant debris promptly Old leaves and crop remains make ideal hiding places for slugs and snails. Despatch them to the compost heap as soon as possible.

Make out seed orders The sooner you order your seeds, the more likely you are to get everything you want; some popular varieties sell out quickly. Keep in mind what crops did particularly well or badly this year when considering what to order for next season.

Keep crops handy In cold areas where the soil might be frozen for prolonged periods, dig up some parsnips, swedes and leeks. Heel them in shallowly in a convenient spot, where they will be easy to lift in cold weather.

Harvest early sprouts Early maturing varieties of Brussels sprouts will be ready for picking this month. Always pick sprouts from the bottom of the stem upwards. Use your heel to firm the plants in the soil if they have been loosened by autumn gales.

Week 1

> **The swallows are long gone and you start to feel that nip in the air – the season is drawing to a close**

Celeriac

Beneath the rather odd, gnarled appearance of celeriac lies delicious, creamy flesh with a subtle, celery-like flavour – but it's far easier than celery to grow.

Celeriac tips

• Sow the tiny seed thinly in pots or modules in early spring to give the crop plenty of time to grow to a good size. Harden off and plant out in late spring or early summer.

• Space the seedlings 30cm (12in) apart in rows 45cm (18in) apart, and water in. Protect from slugs and snails.

• In early autumn, draw soil around the swollen stem-bases to keep the flesh white. On light soil, celeriac can remain in the ground all winter; protect the plants during really cold spells with a covering of straw.

• Choose a position in full sun or partial shade, with well-drained but moisture-retentive soil. Improve the soil's water-holding capacity by digging in lots of organic matter in autumn.

• On heavier ground, and soil prone to waterlogging, harvest in late autumn and store by twisting off the leafy tops and placing the roots in boxes of damp peat or coir in a cool shed.

Recommended varieties

'Monarch' AGM: A smooth-skinned variety with tender flesh, which can be harvested from early autumn.

'Brilliant': Large, round fleshy roots of good quality and excellent flavour.

Week 2

Roasted root vegetable and pumpkin tart

Roasting brings out the sweetness of root vegetables and the pumpkin. You can substitute tasty winter squashes like butternut and acorn squash for pumpkin in any recipe.

Ingredients
Serves 6
600g (1¼lb) pumpkin, seeded
3 parsnips
3 carrots
2 red onions
25g (1oz) butter
1 teaspoon caster sugar
2 tablespoons chopped fresh thyme

5 tablespoons olive oil
ready-cooked savoury shortcrust pastry
  flan case
2 tablespoons whole-grain mustard
2 tablespoons lemon juice
salt and pepper

Method
Preheat the oven to 200°C/400°F/gas mark 6. Cut the pumpkin into 20mm (¾in) chunks, discarding the skin. Cut the parsnips and carrots lengthways into quarters and then widthways in half. Cut the onions into wedges.

Place all the vegetables in a large roasting pan. Add the butter, sugar, thyme and olive oil. Season lightly with salt and pepper and roast in the oven for about 1 hour until golden, tossing the ingredients once or twice during roasting.

Place half the roasted vegetables in a food processor and add the mustard, lemon juice, and salt and pepper. Blend until smooth.

Spread the purée over the pastry case and pile the rest of the vegetables on top. Put in the oven for 10 minutes until heated through. This dish can be assembled several hours in advance and then reheated in a hot oven for 20–25 minutes.

Week 3

> **Growing food is fundamental to human existence**

Clearing, tidying and protecting for winter

There's still plenty to keep you busy at this time of year, even though the days are getting shorter and shorter. Make use of every fine day now to keep the vegetable garden clean and tidy and start preparing for spring.

Clearing and tidying

Plants that have finished cropping should be dug up and added to the compost heap. Don't add anything that is badly diseased, though – spores of diseases like potato blight can survive composting and will spread trouble in future years. Weeds should also be dug up, and many of these can be added to the compost heap, too, though pernicious, spreading weeds such as bindweed and couch grass are best destroyed.

As space becomes vacant in the vegetable garden, start the winter digging. This is a job best done a little at a time to avoid straining your back. Dig in bulky organic matter such as rotted garden compost or farmyard manure as you go, but don't add it to the area where you are going to grow root crops next year.

Neaten grass edges of the vegetable plot by recutting them to a straight line with a sharp edging tool. Maintain paths, removing weeds and topping up with fresh gravel or whatever material is appropriate.

If you have not yet taken down your runner bean supports, do it now. Clean the canes well, and store them in a dry place. You can dip the bases in wood preserver to give them a longer life; they should last several years but tend to become brittle over time.

Protecting winter crops

If you live in a particularly cold area, it might be a good idea to insulate rows of winter root crops that are remaining in the soil, using cardboard, straw, dry bracken or similar materials. This insulating layer should help prevent the ground freezing solid around the roots. In windy areas, peg down a piece of horticultural fleece over the top to keep loose material like straw in place.

Winter brassicas should have any yellowed leaves removed from the base, and if necessary tall plants such as Brussels sprouts can be staked in windy areas. Pigeons are often a nuisance as soon as the weather gets cold; they can ruin a cabbage crop in a few hours. Netting is the only sure way to keep them at bay.

CAROL'S GREEN TIP

CLEAR WEEDY AREAS

Removing weeds and spent crops not only makes the garden look tidier and more pleasing to the eye, it also removes overwintering places for various pests. Slugs and snails are particularly fond of weedy patches and loose leaf litter. Clearing these areas will deprive them of their favourite hiding places, giving you a chance of starting the year without an army of slugs and snails lying in wait.

Week 4

Climate and weather

There's no doubt that life is easier if you garden in one of the milder areas of the country, but even in those favoured parts your garden can have its own microclimate that can make vegetable growing difficult. The weather is one thing we cannot control – but we can reduce its effects. The winter season is a good time to erect fences and plant hedges that can help improve growing conditions.

Wind

Windy conditions slow down vegetable growth and make cloches and horticultural fleece hard to keep in place. Tall plants suffer from wind rock, which loosens the roots; and crops like rows of runner beans, which present a large surface area to the wind, can be flattened by a single storm. Wind also whips moisture away from the leaves of plants in much the same way hot sun does, and leaf scorch is common in windy areas.

Hedges make good windbreaks, being cost effective and good for wildlife; fences are an alternative in small gardens and where quick results are wanted. Porous fences (with 50 per cent gaps) and deciduous hedges are best because they slow the wind, instead of stopping it dead. Solid barriers force the wind up, over and down, creating a damaging buffeting effect on the other side. Special windbreak netting can be bought reasonably cheaply, and this is easy to put up and take down if you need only a temporary windbreak for the stormy months of the year.

Frost

Frosts can be damaging and are worst in low-lying sites where cold air collects. Cold air is heavy, and flows down slopes like water. Gardens at the foot of a hill, or where walls and hedges prevent the cold air from draining away to lower levels, are likely to suffer the worst frosts and are known as frost pockets. Gardens in frost pockets experience a much shorter growing season, and the longer the growing season the better, especially for cold-sensitive plants such as pumpkins and sweetcorn.

If you have the choice, position your vegetable plot partway up a hill, rather than at the base of it. If you are already stuck with a plot in a frost pocket, you may be able to remove barriers like walls which are positioned just below it, to enable the cold air to drain away. You can also construct a wall or fence above the vegetable plot, higher up the slope, and this will hold the cold air back or divert it around the sides.

Left: Badly placed hedges or walls can turn a garden into a frost pocket rather than providing protection.

Compost

Composting can be one of the most rewarding gardening activities, and is good for the environment as well as garden wildlife. In essence, it is just gathering organic waste and allowing natural organisms to break down the waste to a brown, crumbly soil conditioner.

Use two compost bins: one to fill up while the other is rotting down. When you have emptied one, tip or fork the contents of the second into the first bin as a way of turning the heap. If space is short, use small bins, but try to avoid those with a capacity of less than 1cu m (1.3cu yd). Stand them on previously dug-over soil or, if this is not possible, spread a bucketful of soil under the bin. You can even dig a small pit beneath the bin to increase its capacity.

Top left: Most of your garden refuse can be composted and turned into a valuable soil improver.

Top right: Green manure crops can be specially grown for adding to the compost heap.

Bottom: Have two heaps on the go – one to be filled up while the other is rotting down.

What to add to the heap

Add a mix of organic waste from the garden and kitchen to the bin. About a third of the waste should be soft, green nitrogen-rich material such as kitchen waste (like vegetable and fruit peelings) and lawn mowings; the rest should be straw-like or more woody carbon-rich material, such as spent crops. Avoid adding cooked food and meat products, as these can attract rats, and don't add perennial weeds since they will simply grow there, unless thoroughly killed by desiccation first. It is also a good idea to avoid adding diseased material, as disease spores could end up being spread with the compost.

Keep adding waste until the bin is full, adding water if the contents look dry. Then leave them to rot. Turn the heap with a fork, once or twice a year. This can be hard work, but it does speed up the process and improve the results.

CAROL'S GREEN TIP

COMPOST WITH WORMS

Even in very small gardens, worm composting is possible as the bins are small and neat. Worm bins consist of an upper chamber where the waste is added, and a lower sump where liquid collects. The liquid contains plant nutrients and is watered onto growing crops. Eventually the upper chamber fills with compost for the garden, while the worms are recovered for the next batch. Bins and worms can be bought as kits.

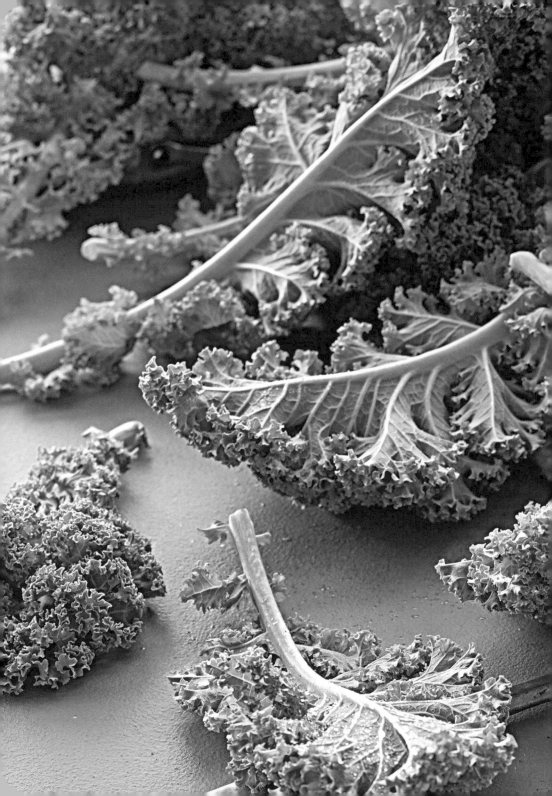

DECEMBER

> The month that contains the shortest day is bound to be a little gloomy, but on the other hand, after the solstice, days begin to draw out, albeit slowly. Spirits can only be lifted by the prospect of longer hours of daylight to come and the feeling that there is the opportunity to start planning for a new year in the vegetable garden.

December is just the start of the winter but that means there are months to get the ground ready and (this is the really exciting bit) work out a strategy for the coming year. Seed catalogues have arrived and some self-indulgent armchair gardening is essential to study them and come up with a plan. Use this journal throughout the year to jot down successes and failures, to record when your crops were sown or planted out and when they yielded their first harvest. How did they perform, and more importantly, how did they taste? Will you grow them again and are there any other varieties you want to try, to extend the season – or just as an experiment?

If there are local varieties you have discovered during the year are you going to try them – and can you find a local source of seed, perhaps at a seed swap? Exchanging seed and sharing it was the practice in the past and it is also going to be the shape of things to come. If you share seed orders with friends and neighbours, everyone benefits and the scope of varieties you can try is exponentially increased. My favourite Christmas present has to be an order of new varieties of potatoes. What a treat in the coming year.

Jobs for December

Get ready for spring Dig over vacant ground, spread organic manures, incorporate green manures, check the pH and add lime if required, and make sure the soil is in the best condition for an early start next spring. It's best to do strenuous jobs like digging little by little to avoid backache and pulled muscles. Leave the soil surface rough to allow frosty weather to work on the clods and break them down; this will make it easier for you to prepare the soil for sowing next spring.

Continue harvesting Gather winter vegetables as required. Where cabbages have been cut, leave the stump in the ground and cut a cross in the top with a sharp knife. Leafy greens will grow from the four corners and can be used later.

Force rhubarb outside Cover rhubarb plants with forcing pots or a large bucket with a stone on top to prevent it blowing away. Seakale can be treated in the same way.

Keep weeding Remove any weeds that continue to appear.

Start using vegetables in store Remove and use up any vegetables that are deteriorating and discard any rotten specimens you come across. Watch out for signs of mice, and take control measures where necessary.

Turn compost heaps Empty compost bins, mix the contents thoroughly and then refill them.

Planning and ordering Draw up plans for next year's vegetable garden. Order seed if you have not already done so. Check you'll have sufficient canes, stakes, netting, fertilizer and cultural controls. Bear in mind that mail-order suppliers and gardening clubs and societies can usually offer significant savings over retail outlets.

Storing seed When your seed order arrives, store it in cool, dark, dry conditions.

Plant rhubarb Plant out new rhubarb crowns and Jerusalem artichoke tubers.

Prepare for indoor sowing Start cleaning seed trays and pots and buy plenty of compost so that you are ready to start sowing early crops under cover.

Week 1

> **By late winter there's an almost irresistible temptation to start sowing and planting**

Turnips

Turnips are sweet and tasty when harvested while still small. An extra bonus is that you can also enjoy the fresh green leaves, or 'turnip tops', with their lovely peppery taste.

Turnip tips

• Turnips do not transplant well and must be sown outdoors directly where they are to grow. Sow small amounts every two weeks or so for a regular supply of young roots.

• Sowing can begin as early as late winter and continue right through to the end of the summer.

• Hot, dry weather may stall seed germination; water the seedbed and shade lightly with netting.

• Flea beetles can pepper the foliage with tiny holes. Keep them at bay by covering the entire crop with horticultural fleece or fine-meshed netting secured firmly round the edges.

• Start pulling turnips when they reach the size of a golf ball, but don't let them develop any larger than a small orange, or they will become woody and much less tasty.

• Turnips are not winter hardy – they will need to be lifted before the cold weather really sets in.

Recommended varieties

'Primera' AGM: Good yields of flat-topped roots with purple tops and attractive smooth skin.

'Oasis': Early, conical white turnips with a sweet, almost melon-flavoured flesh.

Week 2

Buttered cauliflower crumble

Cauliflowers can be grown virtually all year round. In deepest winter, the head can be damaged by frost, but breaking one or two of the uppermost leaves over the developing creamy white curd will help to protect it.

Ingredients
Serves 4
1 large cauliflower
25g/1oz butter
50g/2oz breadcrumbs
2 tablespoons olive oil
3 tablespoons capers
3 cocktail gherkins, finely chopped
3 tablespoons chopped dill or tarragon
100g (3½oz) crème fraîche
4 tablespoons grated Parmesan cheese
salt and pepper

Method
Cut the cauliflower into large florets and blanch in boiling water for 2 minutes. Drain the florets thoroughly.

Melt half the butter in a large frying pan. Add the breadcrumbs and fry for 2 minutes until golden. Drain the breadcrumbs and set aside.

Melt the remaining butter in the pan with the oil. Add the cauliflower florets and fry gently for about 5 minutes until golden. Add the capers, gherkins, dill or tarragon and crème fraîche to the pan. Season to taste with salt and pepper and stir the mixture over a moderate heat for 1 minute.

Turn into a shallow flameproof dish and sprinkle with the fried breadcrumbs and Parmesan. Cook under a preheated moderate grill for about 2 minutes until the crumbs are dark golden brown.

Week 3

> **When you're growing your own vegetables, taste is what counts**

Preparing the soil for next season

Left: Green manure crops may be ready to incorporate into the soil now.

You'll need to dig the vegetable garden to remove weeds and debris, and to incorporate fertilizers, compost and possibly lime to reduce acidity. Even if you intend to follow a no-digging regime later, preliminary cultivation is well worthwhile.

Rotavating a weedy soil to clear it is not a good idea, since the machine chops up the weed roots into many pieces – all of which can take root and regrow. You can remove weeds and their roots by hand while digging; perennial weeds such as bindweed, dandelion, thistles, couch grass and nettles are the ones to look out for. Don't compost but lay them out exposed to sun and wind where they will soon dry out and die.

Adding organic matter

Fertile conditions boost the size, flavour, yield and quality of your vegetables. If you can, add bulky, well-rotted organic matter, such as garden or municipal compost or farmyard manure, every second or third year to half or one-third of your plot. (If you are following a three-year rotation, add manure to the section where you will grow brassicas next season. Do not add it to the root area, as roots can become forked.)

As a rough guide, one bucketful of well-rotted material to every square metre (or yard) is enough, but double this amount could be used for thin, poor soil and for greedy crops.

If you have grown green manure crops, these may be ready to incorporate now. Cut the crops down and let them wilt for a few days before digging them in. Check the pH of your soil (see page 16) and add lime where necessary.

CAROL'S GREEN TIP

NO-DIG GARDENING

There is some evidence that avoiding digging leads to a healthier, more productive soil and for many gardeners it is the only practical way to cultivate clay soil. Clear away weeds and spread organic matter such as well-rotted garden compost over the soil surface in a 2.5–5cm (1–2in) layer. Worms will gradually pull this down and mix it with the soil. In spring, sow straight into the surface layer and cover seeds with further compost.

Week 4

Reviewing the year

It's always interesting – and useful – to look back at the end of the season and see how your growing year has gone. Unfortunately, it's all too easy to forget the details. However, this year you have everything you need – for if you have filled in your weekly journal pages, you should have an excellent record of your vegetable garden's performance.

The important notes to jot down are sowing times, vegetable variety, weather conditions and harvest details – when each crop was ready, and whether it was a bumper yield or a disappointment.

The disappointments might be of most interest, for there is probably more to learn from things that have gone wrong than things that have gone right. If the crop is poor, this might be because you sowed it too late, not giving the plants enough time to develop, or sowed it too early, so that it was damaged by cold weather, or bolted to seed. Weather can play a big part; a cool, damp summer won't be favoured by tomatoes and sweetcorn, and a severe drought might mean far fewer runner beans than normal. There are pests and diseases to consider, too; a heavy infestation of carrot fly might

persuade you to delay your sowings until mid-June next year, to avoid the main carrot fly egg-laying season.

If there is no obvious cultural reason for a poor crop, it may be that you need to try different varieties next year. Scour the seed catalogues for varieties that are described as, for example, resistant to bolting or club root, or grow well in cool conditions – whatever your problem was.

Finally, do take into account whether you actually enjoyed the crops you grew.

Below: Looking back at your successes and failures over the year will give you a idea of what to grow – and to avoid – next season.

GIFTS FOR GARDENERS

Gardeners are among the easiest people to find Christmas presents for! Good garden centres will have all sorts of tempting things, and check out the internet, too. Use your imagination with presentation – say, a selection of vegetable seeds, a trowel and a pair of gardening gloves in a wooden trug; or tomato and basil seeds and a bottle of olive oil in an attractive salad bowl. On a budget, home-made pickles and preserves, made from your home-grown produce, will go down well.

Resources

USEFUL ORGANIZATIONS

Royal Horticultural Society
80 Vincent Square
London SW1P 2PE
Tel: 0845 260 5000
www.rhs.org.uk
A gardening charity dedicated to advancing horticulture and promoting good gardening.

National Vegetable Society
5 Whitelow Road
Heaton Moor
Stockport SK4 4BY
www.nvsuk.org.uk
A charity dedicated to advancing the culture, study and improvement of vegetables, offering help and advice to novice and expert show-grower alike.

Garden Organic
Garden Organic Ryton
Coventry
Warwickshire CV8 3LG
Tel: 024 7630 3517
www.gardenorganic.org.uk
Garden Organic (previously known as the Henry Doubleday Research Association) is an organic growing charity dedicated to researching and promoting organic gardening, farming and food.

National Society of Allotment and Leisure Gardeners
O'Dell House
Hunters Road
Corby
Northants NN17 5JE
Tel: 01536 266576
www.nsalg.org.uk
The aims of the society are to protect, promote and preserve allotment gardening, and to help all to enjoy the pleasures of allotment and leisure gardening.

Organic UK
www.organicgarden.org.uk
An internet-based association offering ongoing support for all organic food growers.

VEGETABLE SEED SUPPLIERS

D. T. Brown & Co.
Bury Road, Kentford
Newmarket
Suffolk CB8 7PR
Tel: 0845 166 2275
www.dtbrownseeds.co.uk

Samuel Dobie & Son
Long Road
Paignton
Devon TQ4 7SX
Tel: 0844 701 7623
www.dobies.co.uk

Mr Fothergill's
Gazeley Road
Kentford, Newmarket
Suffolk CB8 7QB
Tel: 0845 166 2511
www.mr-fothergills.co.uk

S. E. Marshalls & Co.
Alconbury Hill, Huntingdon
Cambs PE28 4HY
Tel: 01480 443390
www.marshalls-seeds.co.uk

Nickys Nursery Ltd.
Fairfield Road, Broadstairs
Kent CT10 2JU
Tel: 01843 600972
www.nickys-nursery.co.uk

Organic Gardening Catalogue
Riverdene Business Park
Molesey Road, Hersham
Surrey, KT12 4 RG
Tel: 0845 130 1304
www.organiccatalog.com

The Real Seed Catalogue
VidaVerde, Brithdir Mawr Farm
Newport near Fishguard
Pembrokeshire SA42 0QJ
Tel: 01239 821107
www.vidaverde.co.uk

Robinson's Mammoth Vegetable Seeds
Sunny Bank, Forton
Nr Preston, Lancs PR3 0BN
Tel: 01524 791210
www.mammothonion.co.uk

Seeds of Italy Ltd.
C3 Phoenix Industrial Estate
Rosslyn Cres., Harrow
Middlesex HA1 2SP
Tel: 0208 427 5020
www.seedsofitaly.com

Suttons Seeds
Woodview Road
Paignton
Devon TQ4 7NG
Tel: 0844 922 2899
www.suttons-seeds.co.uk

Tamar Organics
Cartha Martha Farm
Rezare, Launceston
Cornwall PL15 9NX
Tel: 01579 371087
www.tamarorganics.co.uk

Thompson & Morgan (UK) Ltd.
Poplar Lane
Ipswich
Suffolk IP8 3BU
Tel: 01473 688 821
www.thompson-morgan.com

Edwin Tucker & Sons Ltd.
Brewery Meadow
Stonepark, Ashburton
Newton Abbot,
Devon TQ13 7DG
Tel: 01364 652233
www.edwintucker.com

Unwins Seeds
Alconbury Hill
Huntingdon
Cambs PE28 4HY
Tel: 01480 443395
www.unwins.co.uk

EQUIPMENT SUPPLIERS

Agralan Ltd.
The Old Brickyard
Ashton Keynes
Swindon, Wilts SN6 6QR
Tel: 01258 860015
www.agralan.co.uk
Wide range of products, including horticultural fleece and plant protection mesh, cloches and biological controls.

Agriframes
Tildenet Ltd
Hartcliffe Way
Bristol BS3 5RJ
Tel: 0845 260 4450
www.agriframes.co.uk
Fruit cages, plant supports, fleece, cloches, watering equipment, etc.

Crocus.co.uk Limited
Nursery Court, London Road
Windlesham
Surrey GU20 6LQ
Tel: 0870 787 1413
www.crocus.co.uk
Vegetable plants and seeds, cold frames, cloches, garden tools and equipment.

Ferndale Lodge
Woodview Road
Paignton
Devon TQ4 7NG
Tel: 0844 314 1342
www.ferndale-lodge.co.uk
Wide range of products for the vegetable garden, including polytunnels, pots and trays, tools, raised beds, netting, hessian sacks, fruit cages and cloches.

Green Gardener
Brook Hill, Brundall Road
Blofield, Norwich
Norfolk NR13 4LB
Tel: 01603 716986
www.greengardener.co.uk
Specialists in biological controls, plus stockists of a wide range of environmentally friendly gardening products.

Just Green Ltd.
Unit 14
Springfield Road Industrial Estate
Burnham-on-Crouch
Essex CM0 8AU
Tel: 01621 785088
www.just-green.com
A wide range of environmentally friendly gardening products, including biological controls, compost kits, wormeries and organic composts and fertilizers.

Garden Warehouse
Standroyd Mill
Cottontree, Colne
Lancs BB8 7BW
Tel: 01282 873370
www.lbsgardenwarehouse.co.uk
Wide range of gardening items, including fencing and netting, watering equipment, plant supports, biological controls, organic products, composts, fertilizers, tools and fruit cages.

Growing Success
Unit 1, St Martins Courtyard
Chapel Lane, Zeals
Wiltshire BA12 6NZ
Tel: 01747 841401
www.monrobrands.com/
growingsuccess
Ecological and environmentally sound methods of pest control.

Harrod Horticultural
Pinbush Road
Lowestoft
Suffolk NR33 7NL
Tel: 0845 402 5301
Wide range of products, including raised beds, fruit cages, netting, organic seeds and fertilizers, biological pest control, vegetable storage racks and trugs.

Two Wests and Elliott Ltd.
Unit 4 Carrwood Road
Sheepbridge Industrial Estate
Chesterfield
Derbyshire S41 9RH
Tel: 01246 451077
www.twowests.co.uk
Wide range of gardening products, including greenhouse sundries, cloches, tunnels, frames, propagators and watering equipment.

Sowing and harvesting charts

		Jan	Feb	Mar	Apr	May	Jun	Jul	Aug	Sep	Oct	Nov	Dec
Asparagus	Plant:		•	•	•								
	Harvest:				•	•							
Aubergines	Sow:			•	•								
	Plant:					•	•						
	Harvest:							•	•	•	•		
Autumn cabbage	Sow:			•	•	•							
	Plant:					•	•						
	Harvest:									•	•	•	
Beetroot	Sow:		•	•	•		•	•	•				
	Harvest:						•	•	•	•	•		
Broad beans	Sow:	•	•	•	•						•	•	•
	Plant:			•	•	•							
	Harvest:					•	•	•	•				
Broccoli	Sow:			•	•	•	•						
	Plant:					•	•	•					
	Harvest:	•	•	•	•			•	•	•	•	•	•
Brussels sprouts	Sow:			•	•	•							
	Plant:				•	•	•	•					
	Harvest:	•	•								•	•	•
Carrots	Sow:	•	•	•	•	•	•	•					
	Harvest:	•	•	•			•	•	•	•	•	•	•
Cauliflower	Sow:	•			•	•					•	•	•
	Plant:			•	•	•	•	•	•				
	Harvest:	•	•	•		•	•	•	•	•	•	•	•
Celeriac	Sow:		•	•									
	Plant:				•	•	•						
	Harvest:	•	•	•	•					•	•	•	•
Chicory	Sow:				•	•	•	•	•				
	Plant:					•	•						
	Harvest:						•	•	•	•	•		
Courgettes, marrows, summer squashes	Sow:				•	•	•						
	Plant:					•	•						
	Harvest:							•	•	•	•		
Cucumber	Sow:			•	•	•							
	Plant:					•	•	•					
	Harvest:							•	•	•	•		
Florence fennel	Sow:				•	•	•	•					
	Plant:					•	•	•					
	Harvest:						•	•		•	•		
French beans	Sow:			•	•	•							
	Plant:						•	•					
	Harvest:						•	•	•	•	•		
Garlic	Plant	•	•								•	•	•
	Harvest:						•	•	•				
Globe artichokes	Plant:		•	•	•								
	Harvest:					•	•						
Jerusalem artichokes	Plant:		•	•	•								
	Harvest:	•	•								•	•	•
Kale	Sow:				•	•	•						
	Plant:						•	•	•				
	Harvest:	•	•	•	•	•				•	•	•	•
Leeks	Sow:	•	•	•	•								
	Plant:					•	•	•					
	Harvest:	•	•	•	•					•	•	•	•

		Jan	Feb	Mar	Apr	May	Jun	Jul	Aug	Sep	Oct	Nov	Dec
Lettuce	Sow:			•	•	•	•	•	•	•			
	Harvest					•	•	•	•	•	•	•	
Melons	Sow:				•	•	•						
	Plant: June						•						
	Harvest:							•	•	•	•		
Okra	Sow:			•	•								
	Plant:					•	•						
	Harvest:							•	•	•			
Onions	Plant sets:			•						•	•	•	
	Harvest:					•	•	•	•	•			
Parsnips	Sow:		•	•	•	•							
	Harvest:	•	•	•						•	•	•	•
Peas	Sow:			•	•	•	•						
	Harvest:						•	•	•	•	•		
Peppers and chillies	Sow:		•	•	•								
	Plant:					•	•						
	Harvest:							•	•	•	•		
Perpetual spinach	Sow:				•	•	•						
	Plant:					•	•						
	Harvest:					•	•	•	•	•	•	•	
Potatoes	Chit:		•	•	•								
	Plant:			•	•	•							
	Harvest:						•	•	•	•	•		
Radishes	Sow:			•	•	•	•	•	•	•			
	Harvest:	•				•	•	•	•	•	•	•	•
Rhubarb	Plant:	•	•	•		•					•	•	•
	Harvest:					•	•	•					
Runner beans	Sow:				•	•	•						
	Plant:						•	•					
	Harvest:						•	•	•	•	•		
Spinach	Sow:			•	•	•	•	•	•	•			
	Harvest:					•	•	•	•	•	•		
Spring cabbage	Sow:							•	•				
	Plant:										•	•	
	Harvest:				•	•							
Summer cabbage	Sow:		•	•	•	•							
	Plant:					•	•						
	Harvest:							•	•	•	•		
Swedes	Sow:					•	•						
	Harvest:									•	•	•	•
Sweetcorn	Sow:				•	•	•						
	Plant:					•	•						
	Harvest:							•	•	•	•		
Swiss chard	Sow:				•	•	•	•	•				
	Plant:					•	•						
	Harvest:	•	•	•	•	•	•	•	•	•	•	•	•
Tomatoes	Sow:		•	•	•								
	Plant:					•	•						
	Harvest:							•	•	•	•		
Turnips	Sow:		•	•	•	•	•	•					
	Harvest:					•	•	•	•	•	•	•	•
Winter cabbage	Sow:				•	•							
	Plant:					•	•						
	Harvest:	•	•	•								•	•
Winter squashes and pumpkins	Sow:				•	•	•						
	Plant:					•	•						
	Harvest:							•	•	•	•		

Glossary

ACID SOIL Soil with a pH measurement of below 7, containing no lime or only small amounts of lime. Certain plants such as blueberries are sensitive to lime and will only grow in acid soils.

AGM The Award of Garden Merit is awarded by the Royal Horticultural Society to plants that are judged to be of outstanding all-round excellence.

ALKALINE SOIL Soil with a pH measurement of above 7, containing some lime.

ANNUAL A plant that completes its life cycle in one season.

BIOLOGICAL CONTROL The use of the natural enemies of pests and diseases to control them, instead of chemicals.

BLOSSOM END ROT A disorder causing a shrivelled, blackened area to develop at the base of tomatoes that have not received enough water while the fruits were forming.

BOLTING The premature production of flowers and seed which, in the case of lettuces, for example, makes the leaves taste bitter.

BRASSICA A plant belonging to the cabbage family.

CATCH CROP A quick-maturing crop for growing between the harvesting of one crop and the growing of the next.

CHITTING Allowing potato tubers to form sprouts before planting, usually to ensure an earlier crop.

CLAY Soil composed of very small particles, which is prone to waterlogging, difficult to dig, and slow to warm up in spring.

CLOCHE A low glass or plastic covering used to protect young plants from adverse weather conditions early or late in the season.

COMPOST Garden compost is the decomposed remains of garden waste used as a soil conditioner. Compost is also a proprietary, bagged growing medium for plants in containers.

CONTROLLED-RELEASE, SLOW-RELEASE Describes a fertilizer that releases its nutrients gradually over an extended period of time, according to temperature and soil moisture.

CRUMB Particles of soil clinging together. The smaller the particles, the finer the crumb is said to be.

DAMPING OFF Fungal disease that destroys emerging seedlings by rotting the stems at soil level.

DIBBER Pointed tool used for making holes in soil, ready to receive plants or seedlings.

DRILL Groove or furrow made for sowing seed.

EARTHING UP Drawing up soil around a plant – potatoes, for example – to stop the tubers turning green, or leeks to keep the stems white. Also to help anchor some plants in the ground and stop them rocking in the wind.

ERICACEOUS Describing lime-free or acid soil, or a plant that grows in such soil.

F1 HYBRID Plants or seeds that have been bred under strict conditions to create a crop which is uniform, vigorous and high yielding. Seeds gathered from F1 hybrids will not come true, so you will need to buy fresh stock for the next year.

FLEECE A lightweight, finely woven material laid over crops to protect them against pests or cold weather.

FORCING Growing plants in protected conditions to produce earlier, more tender growth.

GREEN MANURE Plants that are grown specifically to be dug into the soil to improve its structure and fertility.

GROWING BAG A plastic sack of compost intended to be planted directly with vegetables such as tomatoes, usually in a greenhouse or on a patio.

HARDENING OFF The process of acclimatizing tender or half-hardy plants raised under glass to outdoor conditions by gradual exposure to lower temperatures.

HAULM The top growth of crops such as potatoes and peas.

HEEL IN To cover the roots and bases of plants with a shallow layer of soil to prevent them from drying out.

HUMUS Decomposed organic matter in the soil, which improves its water-holding capacity and structure.

INTERCROPPING Growing a quick-maturing crop between slower-growing ones.

JOHN INNES COMPOST A loam-based compost produced to a standard recipe developed by the John Innes Institute in the 1930s.

LOAM A fertile soil that consists of a mixture of clay, sand and organic matter.

MESCLUN A mixture of baby leaves of herbs and vegetables used to make salads.

MODULE An arrangement of small, individual plastic plant pots joined together to fit in a seed tray.

MULCH A thick covering over the soil, usually of well-rotted compost or similar. Its many advantages include locking moisture in the ground in spring by reducing evaporation; insulating the roots of plants in cold winters; blocking out weeds; and improving soil structure.

NEMATODES Small, soil-living, worm-like creatures, some of which cause disease, others of which are useful as biological control agents.

OFFSET Young plant attached to the parent, which can be separated and grown on.

OPEN POLLINATED Plants that are pollinated without special control – in other words, producing non-hybrid seeds.

ORGANIC GARDENING A method of growing plants and promoting soil fertility by natural means, without manufactured chemicals such as insecticides and herbicides.

ORGANIC MATTER Matter derived from anything that has once lived – for example, garden compost produced from plant remains. Plays a valuable part in improving soil structure.

PERENNIAL Persisting for more than two years.

pH A scale used to measure acidity or alkalinity. *See* Acid/Alkanline soil.

PINCH OUT Remove the growing tip by nipping it off with finger and thumb, encouraging the growth of side shoots.

POTAGER An ornamental kitchen garden, mixing flowers and produce.

POTASH Another name for potassium, a nutrient that improves the flowering and fruiting of plants.

POTTING COMPOST Proprietary compost that has been produced for potting up plants after the

seedling stage, containing more nutrients than sowing compost.

RED SPIDER MITE Tiny, sap-sucking spider-like mites that are often found in hot, dry conditions in greenhouses.

RHIZOME A spreading underground stem that looks like a root. Weeds with rhizomes, such as couch grass, are difficult to control as any small piece of rhizome broken off and left in the soil will produce a new plant.

ROSE A fitting for a watering can or hose, which breaks water up into small droplets to avoid damaging plants. A fine rose has very small holes for a delicate spray, while a coarse rose has larger holes for larger droplets.

ROTATION Growing annual vegetables in a different site each season, primarily carried out to prevent the build-up of pests and diseases and to maintain nutrients in the soil.

SEED, RUNNING TO *See* Bolting.

SEED POTATO A potato tuber that is allowed to develop shoots before being planted and growing into a new plant. 'Certified' seed potatoes are guaranteed to be free of pests and disease when supplied for planting.

SEEDBED A specially prepared area of the garden that has been prepared for seed sowing, the soil broken down into very fine crumbs or particles and raked level.

SILT Soil component consisting of fine particles similar to clay.

SOWING AND CUTTING COMPOST Proprietary compost formulated for seed sowing and the rooting of cuttings. It has lower levels of nutrients than potting compost.

STAGING Slatted benching in a greenhouse.

SUCCESSIONAL SOWING Making small sowings at regular intervals to ensure a continuous supply of a crop and avoid one big glut.

TASSELS The silky, thread like male flowers of sweetcorn, which carry pollen to fertilize the female flowers, so producing corn kernels.

TENDER Describing plants that are damaged by cold temperatures.

THINNING Removing some seedlings or plants to make sure that those left are evenly spaced with enough room to grow and can access adequate light and food supplies.

TOP GROWTH The parts of a plant above ground.

TOP SOIL The top layer of fertile soil in which a plant's roots grow.

TRANSPLANT To move a seedling or plant from one place to another for example, a tender seedling from a small to a larger pot or out into the garden. Also (noun) a plant being so moved.

TRUSS A stem carrying a number of regularly spaced flowers or fruits, such as is found on a tomato plant.

TUBER An underground storage organ of a plant, for example a potato or Jerusalem artichoke.

WILT The collapse of a plant, caused by fungal disease or lack of water.

WHITEFLY Very small, white moth-like insect pests common in greenhouses.

Conversion charts

TEMPERATURE		LENGTH		WEIGHT		FLUIDS	
-20°C	-4°F	3mm	⅛in	5g	0.18oz	5ml	0.18fl oz
-15°C	5°F	5mm	¼in	10g	0.35oz	10ml	0.35fl oz
-10°C	14°F	1cm	½in	20g	0.71oz	15ml	0.5fl oz
-5°C	23°F	2cm	¾in	28g	1oz	20ml	0.7fl oz
0°C	32°F	2.5cm	¾in	30g	1.06oz	28ml	1fl oz
1°C	34°F	3cm	1in	40g	1.4oz	30ml	1.05fl oz
2°C	36°F	4cm	1½in	50g	1.76oz	40ml	1.4fl oz
3°C	37°F	4.5cm	1¾in	60g	2.12oz	50ml	1.76fl oz
4°C	39°F	5cm	2in	70g	2.47oz	60ml	2.11fl oz
5°C	41°F	7cm	2½in	80g	2.82oz	70ml	2.46fl oz
6°C	43°F	7.5cm	3in	90g	3.18oz	80ml	2.8fl oz
7°C	45°F	8cm	3½in	100g	3.52oz	90ml	3.17fl oz
8°C	46°F	10cm	4in	200g	7oz	100ml	3.5fl oz
9°C	48°F	12cm	5in	227g	8oz	200ml	7fl oz
10°C	50°F	15cm	6in	300g	10.5oz	300ml	10.56fl oz
11°C	52°F	18cm	7in	400g	14oz	400ml	14.1fl oz
12°C	54°F	20cm	8in	454g	1lb	500ml	17.6fl oz
13°C	55°F	23cm	9in	500g	17.5oz	568ml	1pt
15°C	59°F	25cm	10in	600g	21oz	1l	1.76pt
16°C	61°F	27cm	11in	700g	24.5oz	2l	3.52pt
17°C	63°F	30cm	12in	800g	28oz	4l	7.04pt
18°C	64°F	50cm	20in	900g	31.5oz	4.5l	8pt/1gal
19°C	66°F	75cm	30in	1kg	2.2lb	5l	8.8pt
20°C	68°F	80cm	2½ft	2kg	4.41lb	5.7l	10pt
21°C	70°F	1m	3ft	2.27kg	5lb	6l	10.56pt
22°C	72°F	1.1m	3½ft	3kg	6.61lb	7l	12.32pt
23°C	73°F	1.2m	4ft	4.54kg	10lb	8l	14.08pt
24°C	75°F	1.5m	5ft	5kg	11.02lb	9l	15.84pt
25°C	77°F	1.75m	5⅔in	6kg	13.23lb	10l	2.2gal
26°C	79°F	2m	6½ft	6.81kg	15lb	20l	4.4gal
27°C	80°F	2.5m	8ft	7kg	15.43lb	22.7l	5gal
28°C	82°F	3m	10ft	8kg	17.64lb	30l	6.6gal
29°C	85°F	5m	16ft	9kg	19.84lb	40l	8.8gal
32°C	90°F	10m	33ft	9.08kg	20lb	45.5l	10gal
60°C	140°F	20m	60ft	10kg	22.01lb	50l	11gal

CONVERSION FACTORS

TO CONVERT:

g to oz multiply by 0.035
oz to g multiply by 28.349

kg to lb multiply by 2.205
lb to kg multiply by 0.454

g per sq m to oz per sq yd multiply by 0.0295
oz per sq yd to g per sq m divide by 33.91

mm to in multiply by 0.0394
in to mm multiply by 25.4

cm to in multiply by 0.394
in to cm multiply by 2.54

cm³ to in³ multiply by 0.061
in³ to cm³ multiply by 16.387

litre to pint multiply by 1.76
pint to litre multiply by 0.568

litre to gallon multiply by 0.22
gallon to litre multiply by 4.546

m³ to ft³ multiply by 35.315
ft³ to m³ multiply by 0.028

Index

A
Acid/alkaline soil 16
April 49–62
Artichokes 24, 122
Asparagus 70, 122
Aubergines 44
August 113–26
B
Beetroot 100, 102
Biological control 154
Blanching 136
Blossom end rot 130
Blueberries 120
Bolting 94
Bottling 141
Brassicas 8, 114, 146
Broad beans
  autumn-sown 156
  hints and tips 68
  sowing 160
Broccoli 38
Buttered cauliflower
  crumble 178
Buying
  plants 22, 36, 50
  seeds 31, 160
C
Cabbage 12, 22, 36
Carrots 36, 84, 130
Catch cropping 32
Cauliflowers 8, 178
Celeriac 162
Chit potatoes 14, 174
Chutneys 141, 150
Clay soil 16
Clearing 154, 160, 166
Climate 169
Colcannon recipe 12
Compost
  containers 74
  hints and tips 171
  municipal 28
  November 160
  September 130
Containers
  herbs 46
  hints and tips 74
  for sowing 42
  summer care 126
Conversion charts 190
Corn salad 93
Crowns 36
Cucumbers 44
Currants 120
Curried parsnip soup 26

D
December 173–83
Digging 22, 159, 160
E
Enjoying your garden 110
Equipment 19, 154, 160
F
February 21–32
Feeding 58, 88, 126
Fennel 94
Forcing crops 136
Freezing vegetables 109
Fresh vegetable pizza 134
Frost 66, 169
G
Gap-fillers 106
Garlic 146
Germination rates 36
Gifts for gardeners 183
Gluts 109
Gooseberries 120
Green manures 28, 114
Green tomato chutney 150
Greenhouses
  clearing 154, 160
  February 22
  January 8
  March 42, 44
  May 66
H
Hardening off 50
Harvesting
  charts 186–7
  December 174
  July 98
  June 82
  mature vegetables 138
  October 146
  summer veg 104
Herbs 46, 98
Hot asparagus with balsamic
  vinegar 70
I
Information 184-5
Intercropping 32
J
January 7–19
Job-lists
  January 8
  February 22
  March 36
  April 50
  May 66
  June 82
  July 98

  August 114
  September 130
  October 146
  November 160
  December 174
July 97–110
June 81–94
L
Late-growing
  crops 94
Leeks 10
  recipe 40
Lettuce 93, 98, 130
Loam 16
M
March 35–46
May 65-78
Melons 44
N
Netting 61
No-dig gardens 180
November 159–71
O
October 145–56
Onions 8, 130, 138
Organic matter 28, 180
  see also Compost
  green manures 28, 114
Ornamental veg 125
Overwintering 156
P
Parsnips 22, 26, 146
Pea, lettuce and lemon
  soup 86
Peas 61, 156
Peppers 44, 118
Perennial crops 122
Pests
  April 62
  August 114
  crop rotation 32
  June 82
  March 36
  May 66
pH 16
Pickles 141
Planning
  December 173, 174
  February 30–2
  herb patches 46
Plot preparation 16
Plug plants 77
Potatoes
  blight 98
  chitting 14, 174

Potatoes *continued*
  earthing up 50
  harvesting 130, 138
Pricking out 58
Pumpkins
  Hallowe'en 152
  harvesting 138, 146
  recipe 164
  tips 148
R
Raised beds 142
Regional recipe pots 46
Resources 184–5
Reviews 106, 182–3
Rhubarb 122, 160, 174
Roasted root vegetable and
  pumpkin tart 164
Rocket 93
Rotation of crops 32
Runner beans 114, 146
S
Salads 52, 93, 102
Sandy soil 16
Seasonal check 19
Seed potatoes 8, 14
Seedbed preparation 22
Seedlings 58

Seeds
  buying 31, 160
  early crops 42
  June sowings 82
  late spring 72
  outside sowing 56
September 129–43
Shortcuts 77
Showing 78, 114, 125
Silt soil 16
Slugs 8, 36, 62
Sociable spaces 110
Soil
  December 180
  improving 28
  January 8
  outside sowings 56
  structure 16
  types 16
Sowing 42, 186–7
  see also Seeds
Spinach 52, 94, 98
  recipe 54
Sprouts 160
Storage 104
Strawberries 120
Stuffed peppers 118

Succession 32, 50
Supplies check 19
Supports 61, 82, 120
Sweetcorn 130, 132
T
Terminology 188–9
Thinning out 50, 58
Tidying 154, 160, 166
Tomatoes
  August 114
  chutney 150
  dried 109
  hints and tips 116
  indoor sowing 44
  July 98
  October 146
Tool stores 19
Transplants 50, 66, 106
Tubers 36
Turnips 176
W
Watering 90, 126
Weeds 36, 166
Wind 169
Worms 171

Picture credits

The publishers would like to thank the following for their permission to reproduce the photographs in this book: Marie O'Hara/The Garden Collection 10; Mark Bolton/GPL 14; Stephen Hamilton/GPL 17tr; Jonathan Buckley/The Garden Collection – Great Dixter 18; Jonathan Buckley/The Garden Collection – Design: Virginia Kennedy 19; Mayer/Le Scanff/GPL 24; Nicola Stocken Tomkins/The Garden Collection 31; Liz Eddison/The Garden Collection 33t; Torie Chugg/The Garden Collection 42br; Michael Howes/GPL 44; Derek St Romaine/The Garden Collection – Mr & Mrs Jolley 47t; Andrew Lawson/The Garden Collection 47bl; Nicola Stocken Tomkins/The Garden Collection 47br; Botanica/GPL 61; Derek St Romaine/The Garden Collection 63br; Nicola Stocken Tomkins/The Garden Collection 72tl; Michelle Garrett/The Garden Collection 75tr; Brian Carter/GPL 75b; Torie Chugg/The Garden Collection – Jekka's Herbs 76t; Marie O'Hara/The Garden Collection 79t; Maxine Adcock/GPL 91t; Andrew Lawson/The Garden Collection 104; Nicola Stocken Tomkins/The Garden Collection 107; Nicola Stocken Tomkins/The Garden Collection 111; Liz Eddison/The Garden Collection 120; Gary Rogers/The Garden Collection 123tl; Jane Sebire/The Garden Collection – Dun Ard 124; Roger Benjamin/The Garden Collection 136; Gary Rogers/The Garden Collection 139t; Michelle Garrett/The Garden Collection 139br; Torie Chugg/The Garden Collection – Chateau de la Bourdaisiere 140; Nicola Stocken Tomkins/The Garden Collection 142tl; Jonathan Buckley/The Garden Collection – Design: Bunny Guinness142b; Marie O'Hara/The Garden Collection 152; Juliette Wade/GPL 155; Sunniva Harte/GPL 162; Derek St Romaine/The Garden Collection 168; Michelle Garrett/The Garden Collection 170tl; Derek St Romaine/The Garden Collection 170tr; Derek St Romaine/The Garden Collection 170b; David Cavagnaro/GPL 176; Derek St Romaine/The Garden Collection 180; Liz Eddison/The Garden Collection 182bl; Nicola Stocken Tomkins/The Garden Collection 183